Your Own Private Tuscany

A Guide to Italian Vacation Rentals

Your Own Private Tuscany

A Guide to Italian Vacation Rentals

Lynn Jennings

Note for Librarians: a cataloguing record for this book that includes Dewey Decimal Classification and US Library of Congress numbers is available from the Library and Archives of Canada. The complete cataloguing record can be obtained from their online database at:
www.collectionscanada.ca/amicus/index-e.html
ISBN 1-4120-3945-2
Printed in Victoria, BC, Canada

TRAFFORD

Offices in Canada, USA, Ireland, UK and Spain
This book was published *on-demand* in cooperation with Trafford Publishing. On-demand publishing is a unique process and service of making a book available for retail sale to the public taking advantage of on-demand manufacturing and Internet marketing. On-demand publishing includes promotions, retail sales, manufacturing, order fulfilment, accounting and collecting royalties on behalf of the author.
Book sales for North America and international:
Trafford Publishing, 6E–2333 Government St.,
Victoria, BC v8t 4p4 CANADA
phone 250 383 6864 (toll-free 1 888 232 4444)
fax 250 383 6804; email to orders@trafford.com
Book sales in Europe:
Trafford Publishing (uk) Ltd., Enterprise House, Wistaston Road Business Centre,
Wistaston Road, Crewe, Cheshire cw2 7rp UNITED KINGDOM
phone 01270 251 396 (local rate 0845 230 9601)
facsimile 01270 254 983; orders.uk@trafford.com
Order online at:
www.trafford.com/robots/04-1753.html

10 9 8 7 6 5 4 3 2

"Was it in short, ever well to be elsewhere when one might be in Italy?"
EDITH WHARTON

Acknowledgements

After a number of successful vacations in Italy, staying in rental houses, cooking glorious meals, and roaming around the countryside, people began to ask me for advice on planning their own Italian holidays. This book is the result of taking everything I learned on those trips and putting it all down on paper.

Thanks go out to my fellow travellers, who read the book and offered their constructive comments: Anita Braha, Judy Parrack, Judy Russell, Jane Wolverton and Debbie Zbarsky. Thanks also to my niece Shelley Jennings for her editing expertise, Dianna Colnett for the lovely illustrations, and Avril Orloff for her last-minute design advice.

I couldn't have put it all together without the amazing lay-out and design skills of my favourite travelling companion, Peter Reiner.

TABLE OF CONTENTS

"Life is a combination of magic and pasta."

FEDERICO FELLINI

My Own Private Tuscany: A Typical Day in Paradise

Most days start off in much the same way in our rented farmhouse in Southern Tuscany: I am gently pulled from a delicious slumber by muffled noises in the kitchen and the crowing of the rooster next door. A quick peek behind the curtains reveals another clear, crisp autumn day and the local farmer on his tractor ploughing the field directly beneath my window. As I duck below the windowsill, I catch his friendly wave out of the corner of my eye—I'm glad I brought my flannel pyjamas for these cool mornings!

People are beginning to wander into the kitchen from their rooms (nine of us on this trip). The espresso maker has been filled and a pot of milk has been placed on the stove for *caffelatte*. Someone has sliced the crumbly unsalted Tuscan bread, setting it on the table with sweet butter, fig preserves from the *agriturismo* down the road, and a bowl of the season's last white peaches. Conversation is muted as we struggle to wake up. The first sip of the dark bitter coffee brings us to life and the talk turns to the upcoming day. Someone suggests a hike from Pienza to Montepulciano with a stop for lunch in the striking medieval town of Monticchiello. Others would like to prowl around some of the nearby hill towns, do some shopping, and stop at a rustic inn for lunch. A few are content to stay at the villa, read a book, take a swim and just absorb the silence of the countryside. Slowly we disperse to shower and get dressed.

Four of us have decided to simply jump into one of our tiny rental cars and see where the road takes us. After a brief glance at the map we are on our way. The countryside is just as one imagines it—a postcard-perfect fantasy of hill towns, ancient farmhouses, rolling bare fields (this is autumn, after the grain harvest), and painfully picturesque stands of trees, seemingly planted solely for aesthetic effect. Our first stop of the day is the town closest to our villa, San Quirico d'Orcia, and since this morning's coffee didn't quite remove the cobwebs from last night's multi-course dinner and free-flowing Vino Nobile di Montepulciano, there is no argument when cappuccino at the bar on the main square is suggested. Rejuvenated with caffeine and pastry we wander through San Quirico's quaint streets with its churches and walled gardens, and stop in at a linen shop where we marvel at the vast assortment of jacquard towels and tablecloths, selling at a fraction of the cost of those in specialty shops back home. We make a few small purchases and plan to return for some serious shopping before leaving Italy.

Montepulciano and its weekly roving market is our next stop and when we arrive at 11 a.m. shoppers are already milling about the colourful stalls. Dinner duty has fallen to us this evening and the brimming baskets of fresh produce will dictate what we eat tonight. Porcini mushrooms are in season now but it has been a drier fall than usual, so the local crop is meagre and most of the mushrooms on sale have been imported from Eastern Europe. Nevertheless, this is our one chance to try the fresh version of these legendary *funghi*, so we buy a few hundred grams along with some gorgeous tomatoes, a big bunch of fragrant basil, a couple of fat heads of fennel and some beautiful oranges from Sicily. With a gleam in his eye, the elderly vendor hands me a free gift of *odori*, or soup vegetables, a small bundle containing a carrot, some celery, and a few sprigs of fresh basil and parsley. Fish is next on our shopping list so we wander over to where the vending trucks have gathered and choose the one with the longest queue (always trust the locals when it comes to quality). I know how to identify really fresh fish, but I seldom see it, even in my coastal hometown of Vancouver, British Columbia. And what a surprise to find it here, miles from the sea in Southern Tuscany — fish with crystal clear eyes, scarlet gills, gleaming scales and not a whiff of fishiness. The sardines seem to be calling to us; we buy more than enough for our large group and hand over a paltry six euros. Our booty in hand, we find a stall selling table linens and buy nine inexpensive embroidered cotton dishtowels to use as napkins for the duration of our holiday. We duck into a nearby supermarket for a packet of ice for our fish and head up the hill into town to taste and buy some of the region's world famous wine in the numerous *cantine* lining the streets.

Food shopping always makes me ravenous and as luck would have it, this morning before setting out we made a lunch reservation at a popular trattoria in Pienza, the miniature Utopian city designed by the humanist scholar Piccolomini after he became Pope Pius II (Pienza, formerly Corsignano, was his birthplace). A quick fifteen minutes down the winding road and we arrive just in time to meet the rest of our group for our 1 p.m. reservation. The patron doesn't like his guests to be late and always stresses on the phone, *"L'una e non dopo!"*—One o'clock and not a moment later! We are greeted like old friends as this is our third trip to this simple family-run trattoria and we are shown to a prime table on the terrace under the umbrellas. A menu isn't required—we already know the specialties of the house by heart. I start with *pici al aglione*, a hand rolled pasta with a garlicky, spicy tomato sauce. (How can such a simple combination be this glorious?) We follow with shared platters of roast suckling pig, crispy duck with olives, fried potatoes, zucchini timbales, and an uncomplicated mixed salad, all washed down with carafes of generic *rosso* and *bianco*. Our dessert of choice is *noccioli semi-freddo*, a hazelnut ice cream terrine that we fell in love with at our last meal here, but our waiter insists on also giving us a slice each of the chocolate and the orange versions to try. The bill is surprisingly reasonable for food of this quality; we thank the owners and waddle through the deserted streets of Pienza to our cars.

This is the time of day when the whole country seems to be napping, and with most of the shops and attractions closed, we decide to drive back to the villa to sleep off lunch. But by 4 p.m. I am getting restless and a few of us decide to investigate the hot springs at nearby Bagno Vignone, a tiny spa town popular since the time of the Medici. The ancient pool in the centre of town is no longer open to the public but the town's largest hotel has a huge swimming pool filled with hot mineral water that bubbles directly out of the natural spring. At this time of the year it is mostly Italians "taking the waters" and we have the place almost to ourselves. One of the pools is cool enough for swimming, but our energy is flagging and we are content to just float around, gazing at Rocca d'Orcia, the fortified castle in the distance. After an icy shower I'm shocked to find my appetite returning. Thoughts turn to dinner—we pull into the driveway just as the group is starting to congregate in the kitchen for drinks.

The home crew has been busy setting out plates of olives and thickly sliced wild boar salami, opening bottles of wine and pouring our favourite aperitif, Cynar, a bitter artichoke drink that stimulates the taste buds for the meal to come. Between sips and bites, we swap stories about our day's adventures, and then everyone pitches in to get dinner started. The sardines need to be cleaned; half are destined to be baked, stuffed with fresh porcini mushrooms and bread crumbs; the others will be grilled over hardwood charcoal on the barbecue. Potatoes are cut up for roasting and drenched in lemon juice and olive oil. The fennel and oranges are sliced for a palate-cleansing salad. The giant glass bowl is filled to the brim with sparkling fresh greens from today's market. Fettuccini lightly cloaked in a sauce made from pungent Gorgonzola and farm cream is our first course and somehow it tastes even better on the terrace overlooking the stark Tuscan fields behind the house. We move inside for the *secondi*: the stuffed sardines melt on the tongue and the barbecued sardines drizzled with lemon are eaten with our fingers—heaven. The fennel and oranges are the perfect counterpoint to the slightly oily fish, and the green salad clears the way for dessert: fresh Pecorino cheese from Pienza, drizzled with local honey. Wine and conversation flow freely as we finish our meal with some hazelnut biscotti and *limoncello*, a bracing lemon liqueur, served ice cold. People wander off to bed in dribs and drabs leaving some of the group behind to solve the world's problems. A few pages of my book are all I can manage before I drift off into a blissful sleep.

Substitute your family for my group of friends, reduce your group size to four or just get away with your partner. Add horseback riding, hiking, an art and architecture outing or double up on the pool time—you get the picture. If any of this appeals to you, read on—a memorable vacation in Italy is within your grasp.

ॐ

La Fantasia: An Italian Vacation Rental

If we didn't have the fantasy, we wouldn't buy the books. Authors who write about their adopted homes in Italy feed the dream lives of people like us: armchair travellers who get vicarious thrills from tales of colourful villages and bucolic countryside, with nothing to do but wander and seek out obscure art treasures in ramshackle churches, shop for antiques and fine wines along winding hill town streets, and indulge gluttonous urges: eating tomatoes warm and juicy straight from the garden, sausages made by the farmer down the road, and course after course of delicious food on the terrace of a country restaurant, contemplating the natural beauty of the surroundings. Although most of us would balk at the idea of moving lock, stock and barrel to Italy, a vacation based on this lovely fantasy is well within reach. An enchanting, historic home can be yours for an affordable price (not cheap mind you—this *is*, after all, Italy in the 21st century), renovated with all the modern conveniences, no taxes to pay, no bureaucracy to battle, and only rudimentary Italian skills required. If you crave action and culture, an apartment in the city might be just what you need; if you want to slow down and appreciate the rhythm of rural Italian life, a converted farmhouse in the countryside will give you a true taste of *la dolce vita*. And why limit yourself to Tuscany, an area already so well-trodden by the tourist masses? Italy holds out myriad possibilities for the vacation of a lifetime.

To whet your appetite, here are a few examples gleaned from the thousands of Italian rental possibilities:

Imagine a week staying in a 12th-century castle (restored in the 17th century) in the rolling hills outside of Florence, surrounded by vineyards, olive groves and lemon trees, prices starting at only €700 per week for an apartment for four.
www.montegufoni.it

Practice being lord of the manor (with nine of your closest friends) in a small castle in an Umbrian town complete with a defence tower, a private chapel and 17th-century frescoes, owned by a famous pasta-making family, from €2700 per week. (That works out to only €38 per person, per night!)
www.umbria-rentals.com

How about a small country house in the Venetian lagoon near the tiny island of Burano (with its own motorboat for cruising around the islands), sleeping six to eight, starting at €1500 per week? www.santa-caterina.it

For something a bit more off the beaten path, a getaway for two in Puglia (the heel of Italy's boot) might suit. A week in an authentic *trullo* — the mysterious local stone beehive houses — starts at about €450. www.trullitour.com

If money is no object, you might choose to loll around in a luxury waterfront apartment for six on the Italian Riviera for €6000 per week. The price may seem high until I mention that it includes the use of a 14-metre sailing yacht complete with captain. www.rentvillas.com

Lovers of architecture can rent the massive Villa la Rivella near Padua, designed by Palladio, complete with formal gardens, swimming pool, frescoes, a butler, maids and a cook (price upon request). www.thebestinitaly.com

কৈক

Here is what this guide will and will not do for you. It won't dictate where you should go or stay, what you should see, do or eat, but it will give you all the tools required to custom design a trip that suits your own personality and interests. In the following pages you will find explanations of what to expect in an Italian rental, the reasons that vacation rentals are vastly superior to hotels, and specific instructions for finding a rental on the Internet at a price *you* can afford. There are descriptions of regions to visit, the probable costs involved in renting, and tips on car rental, driving, and travelling with groups and children. Instructions on dining out and shopping in family-run stores, supermarkets and outdoor markets are spelled out for you. You'll even find reviews of rental agencies and guidebooks, and cookbook recommendations to help you prepare superb meals.

কৈক

Is a Vacation Rental the Right Choice for your Holiday?

Renting in Italy is not for everyone. It is important to be honest with yourself when considering whether you should rent or stay in a hotel (and don't forget, you can always do a combination of both). If this is your first trip to Italy, and you are trying to get a broad overview of the country in a short period of time, a hotel is your only real option as most rentals require a seven-day minimum stay. Ask yourself the following questions or give this list to any potential travelling companions:

If you:

- Need champagne and a clubhouse sandwich from room service at
- 2 a.m.;
- Have a phobia about flying and crawling insects;
- Can't start your day without a 20-minute hot shower;
- Frequently operate a hair dryer and a curling iron at the same time;
- Insist on fresh towels and sheets every day;
- Do not like the sound of church bells, farm equipment, barking dogs or roosters;
- Require a concierge to help plan your every move;
- Haven't made your own bed in years;

Then an Italian vacation rental may not be for you. Please pass this book on to a friend.

If on the other hand you:

- Find the routine of the average tourist somewhat dull;
- Like to interact with the locals and experience the rituals of daily life;
- Want to look beneath the surface when you travel;
- Are as interested in spending a day pursuing the *dolce far niente* as in rushing around taking in the sights;
- Love to shop at local markets and cook regional specialties in your own kitchen;
- Think that difficulties encountered along the way are simply fodder for a funny story;

- ❧ Adore the smell of clothing dried on a clothesline;
- ❧ Don't like to wake up in your hotel bed with a chocolate stuck to your back because you failed to notice it on your pillow;

Congratulations! You are the perfect candidate for a vacation rental. Make a reservation, book your flight, and pack your bags.

Do I need to speak Italian?

I have never met anyone who claimed that travel in Italy was difficult because they didn't speak the language. Many Italians speak at least some English and are also adept at making themselves understood through the international language of hand gestures and facial expressions. They don't expect tourists to speak Italian but it is a matter of common courtesy to learn a few words before your departure, even if they are as basic as *grazie, prego, scusi,* and *per favore*. A good phrase book will help you in all but the stickiest situations. If you do spend some time in Italy, you will likely want to learn more—the language is melodic and expressive and fun to speak. Why not take a course through continuing education at your local university or community college, or pick up a book and some tapes from the library?

The Advantages of Vacation Rentals over Hotels

Cost

Consider this: A double room in a standard three-star hotel in Florence now costs between €150 and €200 per night. What do you get for that price? A small bedroom with an attached bathroom, and a scanty breakfast of coffee, bread, and jam. Starting at about €800 *a week* you can rent a small apartment with a double bedroom, a dining room, a sitting room with a sofa bed for two, and a kitchen or kitchenette with a stove, coffee maker and washing machine. When you factor in the money you would save by eating even a few meals in the apartment—Italian restaurants are notoriously expensive and the breakfast that is included in the price of your hotel always costs more than what you could make yourself or even find at a local café—the savings can be substantial. Of course, if you can afford to pay more, you can find some very grand properties for rent in Italy complete with frescoes, stunning views, and a small army of staff. In truth, everyone from the most cost-conscious traveller to those who are able to afford all the luxuries will find something to satisfy their needs.

Space

Staying in a hotel in Italy, particularly in the larger cities, is a claustrophobe's nightmare. Real estate prices are high and hotel rooms are tiny. The only place you will have room to really stretch your limbs is the hotel lobby, where you lose all privacy. With a rental you will have room to breathe, spread yourself out, and make yourself at home.

Comfort

A vacation isn't simply about being a tourist—sometimes you want to take a day off from the rounds of churches, museums and shopping to just relax and decompress. Have you ever tried to spend a whole day in a hotel room? Inevitably, just as you are settling in with your novel (or drifting off for a mid-morning nap) housekeeping stops by to clean, and within a couple of hours the walls are starting to close in. With a rental there is a comfy sofa to flop down upon, a kitchen in which you can prepare lunch or a quick snack, and likely even a pool for a refreshing dip. You can lounge around for the entire day in your pyjamas if you like. Somehow just being in your own space gives you greater permission to spend the day reading or dreaming, and removes the compulsion to rush around.

Cooking and eating

Many Italians would agree with me when I say that the best food in Italy is home cooking. Not that restaurant cooking is bad, quite the opposite, but there is a sameness to it. Restaurants in a single region will usually serve slight variations in a repertoire of about twenty typical dishes. When you have your own kitchen, the sky is the limit—a wonderful array of fruit and vegetables, fresh fish, meat and poultry, cured pork products, cheese, and fine wines is readily available in small shops, supermarkets, and open air markets. Italian food is simple to prepare, emphasizing good ingredients, not elaborate preparation. And besides, almost anything tastes good tossed with pasta. Even non-cooks can take advantage of the delicious prepared foods available in supermarkets and delicatessens.

Pack lightly—unpack once

Most rentals have a washing machine either in the unit or somewhere in the complex. Larger cities have laundromats and smaller towns and villages will usually have a *lavanderia* where you can take your laundry and have it washed for you. This allows you to travel with a small suitcase and only one week's clothing, making it much easier to negotiate getting in and out of taxis, trains, and cars, and allowing you to carry your luggage on the plane with you. My husband maintains that there are only two kinds of luggage: carry-on and lost. Once you arrive at the rental you can unpack once and forget about it—no rushed repacking to catch the next train, no rummaging in the bottom of your suitcase looking for a wayward sock.

Ideal for groups

If you have ever tried to organize a large group of family or friends all staying in the same hotel (or even worse, staying at separate hotels) then you will know that the logistics of tracking people down and gathering them in one place can be a nightmare. Having to spend most of your time together in hotel lobbies and restaurants does not provide you with the opportunity to really enjoy and appreciate each other's company. Renting a large house offers the perfect balance of privacy and togetherness, leading to a greater sense of camaraderie—likely the reason you planned this special vacation in the first place.

Live like a local

My guess is that most people reading this book consider themselves "closet" Italians. There is something remarkably seductive about the place that Italy inhabits in the popular imagination. Much of it is cliché: the grandmother in the house dress stooped over a simmering pot of tomato sauce; large groups of family gathered under a grape arbour eating huge meals and drinking home made wine (these days grandma is either at work or on a cruise and the big family is just too busy to get together except on important holidays), but we still admire the way that Italians seem to understand what is really important in life and envy their unmistakable *joie de vivre*. This is your chance to try being Italian, even for a week or two. Leave your cares (and your diet) behind. Surround yourself with the sights, sounds and tastes of one of the most vibrant countries in the world.

A brief word about the advantages of renting over buying

The recent rash of books about people buying and restoring homes in Italy would have you believe that there is a simple recipe for success: find and fall in love with a pile of crumbling old rocks, negotiate a fair price with a shady, but kind-hearted real estate agent, and hire a crew of picturesque local workers to perform the renovations. Throw in a few minor slapstick catastrophes for comic relief and within a few short months you can start your storybook life as an adopted Italian, surrounded by legions of adoring friends and neighbours. These books don't tell you about Italy's strict residency requirements, the extremely high cost of real estate, renovation, and home maintenance, and the quagmire of the Italian bureaucracy. Unless you have an unlimited supply of ready cash or have decided that you are going to apply for Italian residency and live full time in Italy and have some way of making money once you get there (no easy task, by the way) you will always be better off renting than buying. This conclusion holds even if you are able to spend a few months a year in Italy. If you rent, a house that you could normally only dream about owning can be all yours, if only for a luscious week or two.

Types of Vacation Rentals

Apartment in the city

If you are a culture hound, love to eat in fine restaurants, and wish to avail yourself of the shopping opportunities that Italy presents, renting an apartment in the city is for you. Amenities and services abound and you can manage your vacation on foot or by taxi and public transit. Florence, Rome and Venice are the obvious choices but don't overlook the charm of smaller cities like Bologna, Trieste, Verona and Perugia. Intrepid travellers might even consider renting in Naples or Palermo. Wherever you end up, remember that visiting an Italian city doesn't give you the complete scope of what is available in this incredibly diverse country—the occasional day trip to the countryside is *de rigueur*.

A couple of important considerations: Location *is* important—do some research on the city and seek out the most desirable neighbourhoods, ideally close to restaurants, shops and transportation. If you are bothered by noise your rental should be a respite from the constant din—avoid main roads or busy piazzas and look for an apartment on a courtyard or side street. Always travel with earplugs. To assure a good night's sleep consider renting just outside of town within a short bus or train trip to the city centre.

Apartment or house in a small town

Those who like to be less anonymous on vacation and want to experience some real Italian village life should consider renting in a small town. You have the opportunity to be greeted as a regular at the local coffee bar or grocery store and the pace will suit someone who doesn't want the hustle and bustle of the city but, still wants to be close enough to amenities for convenience. A car for tooling around the countryside is a must since most of these towns will not have enough to keep you occupied for a week or two. Non-drivers should choose a town on a main train line or with regular bus service to neighbouring towns or cities.

Apartment in the country as part of an estate, *borgo* or castle (including *agriturismo*)

Many of the rentals you will find in Italy will be located in farm buildings, castles or small *borghi* (villages) that have been renovated into a number of small apartments with all the modern conveniences. *Agriturismi*, which are farms or agricultural estates that offer apartments to paying guests, also fall into this category. There is generally an on-site caretaker or owner to handle check-ins and maintenance, and there may be a restaurant or at least a small shop selling products like wine and jam produced on the premises. Swimming pools and laundry facilities are shared by all of the suites and many of the complexes cater to families with children. These types of rentals tend to be reasonably priced and have numerous amenities like tennis courts, bicycle rentals and on-site cleaning staff. Management and maintenance people are on call if you have any problems. Some are even able to organize group activities and day trips. These advantages are counterbalanced by a certain lack of privacy, noise (particularly if family-oriented), and small, minimally equipped kitchens or kitchenettes.

Apartment in a resort area

Italians flock to beach resorts in July and August. As a result, prices are high, reservations are difficult to come by, and the beaches are unpleasantly crowded. But once September arrives everyone returns home and the prices roll back. Just remember that many resort restaurants and shops close down from about November until April—your winter dining and shopping choices may be limited.

Stand-alone house in the countryside

For those seeking privacy, peace and quiet, and a real sense of Italian "ownership", a house in the country is my pick for the ultimate rental. A dwelling of this kind can range from a renovated chicken coop for two to a renaissance castle for thirty. The choices are mind-boggling but the relative popularity of this type of rental demands an early reservation. It is a plus if the owner or caretaker of the house lives nearby—you will need someone to call if you have any problems. If relative isolation and a good night's sleep are a priority ask about the proximity of neighbours and the location of major roads.

Home exchange

Home exchange can be a fascinating and inexpensive way to take a holiday, especially if you have children or don't mind travelling during July and August, when most Italians take their vacations. Keep in mind that finding an exchange is much easier if you live in a desirable area and if you are somewhat flexible with your dates. You are more likely to find someone who lives on the outskirts of Florence wishing to go to San Francisco than to Moose Jaw, Saskatchewan. I have never managed to organize an exchange myself, but friends have told me that their home exchanges were some of their most successful vacations. A home exchange agency can also be a good source for inexpensive rentals—many of the exchangers offer their second homes at the seashore or in the countryside for rent. The following agency, Intervac, has been in business for over 50 years and is a good place to start:

INTERVAC INTERNATIONAL HOME EXCHANGE HOLIDAY SERVICE

Intervac Canada
606 Alexander Cr. N.W.
Calgary, AB T2M 4T3 Canada
Fax: 403-284-3747
E-mail: sc@intervac.ca
Web: www.intervac.ca

Intervac US
30 Corte San Fernando
Tiburon, CA 94920 USA
Toll-free: 800-756-HOME
E-mail: info@intervacus.com
Web: www.intervacus.com

Intervac International: www.intervac.com

&-6

La Bella Italia: Where to Go

While Tuscany is likely the first place that enters your mind when you think about a vacation rental in Italy, I urge you not to limit yourself to this beautiful, but increasingly popular tourist destination. Great food, stunning scenery and extraordinary cultural attractions are found everywhere in Italy. Here are a few brief words on some of Italy's regions to entice you to travel further afield on your next trip:

Abruzzo and Molise

Italy's last real wilderness; national parks; unhurried pace; villages virtually unchanged for centuries; cold clear water used in making the country's best pasta
www.regione.abruzzo.it/turismo

Apulia (Puglia)

Warm hospitality in the "heel of the boot"; the conical stone *trulli* houses of Alberobello; Baroque architecture of Lecce; olives and *orecchiette* (little ears) pasta
www.itineraweb.com/english/index.html

Campania (Campagna)

The chaos and faded splendour of pizza's birthplace, Naples; Roman ruins in Pompeii and Herculaneum; *mozzarella di bufalo*; the Amalfi Coast, Positano and Capri (impress the locals and say CA-pri, not ca-PRI)
www.medivia.it/inglese/index.htm

Emilia Romagna

Bologna "The Fat", home of the best food in Italy; the Adriatic Coast; prosciutto and Parmigiano-Reggiano from Parma; fine wines; balsamic vinegar from Modena
www.emiliaromagnaturismo.it/english/index.asp

Friuli Venezia Giulia

Undiscovered by tourists; bordered by Austria, Slovenia and the Adriatic; the vibrant capital of Trieste, the "Vienna" of Italy; *Prosciutto di San Daniele* and strudel
www.turismo.fvg.it

Lazio

Etruscan ruins; the Vatican City and the Pope; the splendours of ancient Rome; the beguiling villages of Sperlonga and Ladispoli; a respite from Rome in the pastoral countryside of the Castelli Romani
www.deliciousitaly.com/lazio.htm

Liguria

Jagged coastline and rocky coves; painfully chic Portofino; rough and ready Genoa; hiking in the Cinque Terre; pesto and seafood
www.turismo.liguriainrete.it

Lombardy (Lombardia)

The sophisticated fashion mecca of Milan; Da Vinci's ruined folly *The Last Supper;* boating on Lake Como and Lake Garda; walking in the footsteps of Stradivari in Cremona; *osso buco,* and *risotto Milanese* made with Italy's best rice
www.lombardia.indettaglio.it/eng/turismo/turismo.html

The Marches (Le Marche)

Tourist-free; friendly prices; seaside resorts; truffles and porcini; Piero della Francesca's masterpiece, *The Flagellation of Christ* in Urbino
www.le-marche.com

Piedmont (Piemonte)

Elegant and sophisticated Turin; Barolo and Barbaresco wines; white truffles from Alba; antiques, palaces and Spumante in Asti; Lago Maggiore and Lago d'Orta
www.regione.piemonte.it/lingue/english/index.htm

Sardinia (Sardegna)

Italy for the adventurous: mountains and gorges, deserted beaches, chic resorts, unpolluted seas, aquamarine water; sheep, sheep and more sheep
www.sardegnaweb.it

Sicily (Sicilia)

Well-preserved Greek ruins (better than Greece); Baroque and Moorish influence in exotic Palermo; couscous, *cannoli,* and pistachio ice cream on brioche; proud independent people
www.bestofsicily.com

Trentino - Alto Adige

Austria or Switzerland with an Italian accent; castles galore; skiing, hiking and climbing in the Dolomites; gentle prices; robust and filling cuisine: dumplings and *lasagna al forno*
www.hallo.com

Tuscany (Toscana)

Art treasures of Florence and Siena; strolling in elegant Lucca; Brunello di Montalcino; the vineyards of "Chiantishire"; San Gimignano's towers; *bistecca alla Fiorentina* and bruschetta; shopping for Gucci and Prada
www.turismo.toscana.it/ttgg/htmle/ttidgge.htm

Umbria

Italy's "Green Heart"; the vibrant hill towns of Gubbio, Spoleto and Todi; art treasures and St. Francis in Assisi; pottery in Deruta; chocolate in Perugia
www.bellaumbria.net

Veneto

Beautiful, crowded, exasperating Venice, *La Serenissima*; the architectural gems of Palladio in Vicenza; Romeo and Juliet in Verona; risotto and *baccalà* (salt cod)
http://turismo.regione.veneto.it/index.phtml?=en

∽

The Best Time to Travel

In my experience, spring and autumn have a slight edge over summer and winter, but a holiday in Italy is one of life's great pleasures any time of the year.

Spring

Ah, *primavera*, my favourite season for Italian travel: the weather is gentle, warm but not yet sizzling, wildflowers are in bloom, and the crowds in the cities are not too oppressive (although you shouldn't fool yourself into thinking that the big cities will be crowd-free—you can still wait for two hours to get into the Uffizi gallery in Florence at the beginning of May). Prepare yourself for rain and some very cold days at the start of the season and take a warm sweater or wrap to wear in your rental on cool evenings. There may be a fireplace you can light to take the edge off the chill.

Summer

Italians take *their* vacations during the summer months, so if you travel to a beach resort in mid-summer, you will meet many locals on holiday. In a similar vein, if you want to experience quieter than average cities go to Rome, Florence, or Venice at the same time. Children will love staying in multi-apartment complexes in the countryside where they can meet other kids from all over Europe and North America. At this time of the year I would recommend spending the extra money required to obtain a property with a swimming pool or air conditioning (but even without air conditioning, the thick stone walls will keep the house relatively cool as long as you keep the windows and shutters closed during the day).

Autumn

This is a lovely season, too. Temperatures moderate again in September and October, the crowds have thinned, and the grape harvest is in full swing. Nights can be chilly in October—find a rental with a fireplace for those cooler evenings (in some areas central heating is banned from April to November).

Winter

In winter you share Italy with the Italians—the tourist hordes go home and the cities and towns are returned to the locals. Restaurant reservations are easy to come by and line-ups at tourist attractions are almost non-existent. Unless you are seeking solitude and quiet days spent reading by the fire it might be better to rent in the city—it is certainly one of the best times to see normally overcrowded Venice. Heating is a must at this time of year and can be very expensive—seek out a rental that includes heating in the price.

The Nitty Gritty: How Much Will it Cost?

L et's face it—Italy is one of the most expensive countries in the world. A clerk at a currency exchange in Florence recently told me that when the Euro was introduced many businesses simply saw it as an opportunity to increase their prices. Some hotels charging 200,000 *lire* per night (equivalent to about €100 at the time) started charging €200—a 100% increase! There are no real bargains, but a vacation in Italy needn't be too financially damaging. You really need to analyze your prices based on a per person cost, not on the property cost. €2500 per week may sound expensive, but if divided between eight travellers it is only about €44 per day. Obviously if you are a rock star or an heiress you will probably choose to pay a lot more—houses can be rented with cooks, drivers and maids, but frankly this shields you from the culture and keeps you from doing the things that make renting so appealing in the first place.

Here are some sample budgets for a rental property in Tuscany in the mid-season (April to mid-May and late September through October), exclusive of airfare, to give you an idea of costs. Both are based on having your evening meal in the villa—if you choose to eat all your meals in restaurants add another €25 – €40 per day. As always, adjust prices up or down to compensate for the season and region. I haven't included a budget on the high end—simply take one of these sample budgets and add as many zeros as you can afford.

Modest trip for four

This budget is based on the **per person, per day** cost for a two-bedroom, one-bathroom apartment in an *agriturismo* (pages 12-13) or apartment complex, without a dishwasher or in-suite washing machine.

Apartment rental (€800/week)	€28
Car rental (2-door Fiat Punto or similar)	€10
Picnic lunch or sandwich	€10
Groceries and gasoline	€15
Miscellaneous (coffee, newspaper, admission fees)	€15
Total	€78

Moderate trip for eight

Based on the **per person, per day** cost of a freestanding villa with four bedrooms, two bathrooms, a dishwasher and a washing machine.

Villa rental (€2800/week)	€50
Car rental (2 x Alfa Romeo 4-door or similar)	€15
Restaurant lunch	€25
Groceries and gasoline	€20
Miscellaneous (coffee, newspaper, admission fees)	€20
Total	€130

At the time of printing, the exchange rates for the Euro were:

1 Euro = 1.56 Canadian dollars
1 Euro = 1.20 US dollars
1 Euro = 0.67 British pounds
1 Euro = 1.74 Australian dollars
1 Euro = 1.86 New Zealand dollars

For current rates, check the Universal Currency Converter at **www.xe.net/ucc.**

We're Not in Kansas Anymore, Toto: The Realities of an Italian Rental

Northamericans are often surprised (and befuddled) when confronted with Italian kitchens, plumbing, electricity, lighting and beds. Knowing what to expect will help you avoid confusion and disappointment.

Beds and bedrooms

Most Italian vacation rentals started their life as something else: a farmhouse that sheltered animals on the ground floor with the family living above, a tobacco drying shed, or even a stable. As a result, many rental properties do not have typical bedroom sizes and configurations. Something listed as a single bedroom on a website may in fact be a single bed in a hallway or a bed on an open mezzanine. Always check to see if the bedrooms are separate and private, meaning you don't have to walk through one bedroom to get to another. This may be fine for a family group but is probably less suitable for a group of adults travelling together. Floor plans are very useful in determining layout and many agencies are starting to include them on their websites.

Single beds are very narrow—active sleepers beware! A king-size bed is often two single mattresses pushed together, giving the owner of the house greater options for rental configurations, but forcing you to "mind the gap". On a couple of occasions I have awakened precariously sandwiched between two beds, inches from the floor.

A rental listing that says "sleeps 4 + 2" doesn't necessarily mean that the rental comfortably sleeps six. The "+2" in the description is usually a sofa bed, which I like to call the *letto del morto* or "bed of death". Save this instrument of torture for occasional overnight guests or children and teenagers with very malleable backs.

More and more owners are furnishing their rentals with proper orthopaedic mattresses, but there are still many soft, lumpy beds out there—if you have back trouble you should always inquire about the condition of the mattresses.

Electricity and lighting

Electricity in Italy is very expensive and the supply in your rental (even a pricey one) may seem inadequate. You often can't run more than one appliance at a time without blowing a fuse. Always ask the owner or caretaker for the location of the fuse box so you can switch a fuse back on yourself without assistance.

Bedroom and kitchen lighting is very low and many bedrooms lack reading lamps or have lamps with low wattage bulbs, making it almost impossible to read. I like to take a small light that clips onto a book, or a camping headlamp, which is also invaluable for night time barbecuing.

The electricity in Italy is 220 volts. Canadians and Americans should carry dual voltage appliances and an adapter or a converter and adapter. The plugs are the standard round European two-prong version, though many outlets now require grounded plugs. Adapters for these are available in any Italian hardware store for a few euros. The website **www.kropla.com** has a World Electric Guide with further information and pictures of Italian plugs.

As a courtesy to the owner always turn off any lights that you are not using and turn off all the lights when you leave the house for the day.

Plumbing

I don't know much about plumbing but I can tell you that Italian plumbing is a mystery. Run water in the bidet and the shower pan fills with water. Flush the toilet and the floor shakes. Showers can be notoriously slow to drain. Always look down regularly when you are taking a shower to make sure that you are not flooding the bathroom floor (and the ceiling below).

Kitchens

Your rental kitchen will probably not be equipped with a microwave oven, an American-style coffee maker, a food processor, a toaster, or fancy knives, but will always come with a large pot for cooking pasta, a *moka* (a two-part stove-top pot for making espresso), and plenty of small white cups. Refrigerators are usually quite small, necessitating daily shopping trips. Many rentals will have a couple of burners but no oven—confirm this with the agency if you think you might want to do some roasting or baking.

Unless the house is missing something essential like adequate plates and cutlery or basic pots it is not up to the owner to provide them. A trip to the hardware store will solve your problem easily—you can either leave the item behind as a gift to the house or take it home as a souvenir. The ecologically minded can stop at a local market to buy inexpensive dishtowels to use as cloth napkins, a lovely reminder of your trip when you dry your dishes back home. You may choose to bring along one good knife (in checked baggage, of course).

Screens

For some reason, Italians are not fond of screens on their windows. If you are travelling in late fall, early spring, or winter this won't be a problem but at other times of the year you may wake up covered in insect bites. DEET, mosquito coils, and a little plug-in contraption that sends out a chemical repellent are readily available at hardware stores in Italy. If you are very sensitive to mosquito bites and prefer a less toxic solution, most travel specialty stores in North America carry folding mosquito nets. The property description will likely list the presence of screens. If you don't have them you can deter insects by leaving the windows closed until you turn off the lights at bedtime.

Furniture

Furniture in a vacation rental can range from high-end antiques and family heirlooms to cheap cast-offs. Personally, I prefer furniture that is not too fancy—expensive antiques make me nervous and I am afraid of inadvertently damaging a valuable keepsake. At least one comfy sofa for reading or taking a nap is an absolute must. Some less expensive rentals and *agriturismi* will not have a proper living room but will have a couple of chairs or a sofa in the corner of the kitchen (the main living area in a traditional Tuscan house). Pictures on a website or in a catalogue should give you this information—if you don't see a living room, don't assume that one exists.

Telephones

Most vacation rentals are not equipped with telephones although many agencies offer the option of renting a cell phone for the duration of your stay. This is worthwhile for making restaurant and museum reservations, for ease of communication within larger groups, and for emergencies. If you don't have a phone or cell phone you will need to use pay phones, which are becoming harder to find as cell phones proliferate. You can buy a phone card with a set limit at small shops called *tabacchi*. Break off the corner of the card where indicated, insert it into the slot on the pay phone and dial. Be sure to call your local phone company before you leave home to get the number in Italy for your home country's direct line—they change frequently.

৯৫৯

Safety

Italy is a very safe country and violent crime is rare, but unfortunately property crime and petty theft are rampant. There is no cause for alarm. If you follow a few simple guidelines your vacation need not come with any nasty surprises.

Never leave anything in your car (and I mean never). Vehicles are broken into all the time and nothing is more disheartening than having your luggage or recent purchases stolen. Locking your stuff in the trunk doesn't help, especially if you take the time to open it and stash your belongings in plain view of the criminals lurking around the parking lot.

Keep your passport, credit cards and money with you at all times unless you have a safe in your rental property. Keep the villa or apartment locked even if you are just going outside to sit by the swimming pool. I know of someone whose valuables were pilfered from their villa while they sunbathed only yards away.

Don't hang your purse on the back of a chair in a restaurant or place it on the seat beside you. Snatch and grab artists are very adept at stealing your bag and escaping before you have time to notice.

Don't put your luggage in the baggage area at the end of a train car. Even on deluxe EuroStar trains you should always use the rack directly above your seat. On our last trip to Italy one of our friends saw a thief snatch her bag at a brief stop, jump from the train, throw the bag down a blind staircase (he probably thought he could retrieve it later), and escape through the station. She leapt off the train after him and managed to recover the bag and get back on the train just before it departed. Most of us would not be as lucky (or intrepid) and no one needs that kind of high drama while on vacation.

Avoid having that vacant lost tourist look. Always look as though you know what you are doing and where you are going. Do not walk around with an open map in one hand and a guidebook and camera in the other. Plan your route ahead of time.

ॐॐ

Some Notes on Travelling with Groups

My most enjoyable holidays in Italy have been with groups of seven to ten people. The diversity of personalities, the opportunity to break into small groups to explore the countryside and, most of all, the wonderful conversations over good food and wine late into the evening satisfy my version of the Italian fantasy vacation. With a little advance planning and an abundance of open communication a trip such as this can be a joy.

The planning process

Planning a trip like this can be daunting. Once you have put your group together (be sure to give each person the checklist on page 7), I recommend at least three organizational meetings starting nine months to a year before you plan to travel. During the first meeting you should discuss your destination, the type of property you wish to rent (one large villa or a couple of smaller apartments), your tentative travel dates, a realistic budget, and general expectations for the trip. Appoint a group leader who will be responsible for tracking finances, organizing meetings, communicating with the villa owners, and assuring that each person fulfills their delegated responsibilities. Ask the group leader to research at least five potential rental properties for presentation at the next meeting or ask each group member to research and present one or two.

The second meeting should ideally follow within a few weeks and no longer than a month after the first. Present your prospective rentals and discuss the various options with the group. Choose one favourite and two fallback options and confirm your travel dates. The group leader should now contact the agencies or owners to check availability on the pending choices. Do a survey via telephone or e-mail to finalize your choice and collect a deposit from the members.

Use an e-mail or telephone reminder to collect the final payment, usually due about 90 days in advance. This is also a good time to reserve your rental cars (page 54). Three weeks to a month before you leave, reconvene the group to hammer out the final details: decide where to meet, designate your primary and secondary drivers (and remind them to get an International Driver's Licence) and exchange flight and hotel information. Give copies of the villa rental contract, the car rental contract, and directions to the rental to each group member and make sure they all have their travel documents in order. Passports must be valid for 6 months *past* the date of entry. Divide up guidebooks, reading material, and maps. This is a good time for participants to voice any concerns they may have about practically anything.

I am often asked how we manage cancellations on a trip like this. If price is no object, the group can simply absorb the cost of the person who cancels. That is not my situation, nor the situation of the other cost-conscious people with whom I travel. Our policy is this: Once you have committed and paid, money will not be refunded unless a replacement (approved by the group) can be found. In concert with this policy, we encourage everyone to buy cancellation insurance, and you should as well.

Tips for a successful group vacation

Don't rent one large vehicle or van for transporting your group unless you are a family or have only one qualified driver. This means you will have to go everywhere and do everything together, a recipe for certain disaster. In fact, smaller is always better when it comes to renting a car in Italy, as large vans cannot negotiate the narrow village roads and two small cars are almost always cheaper to rent than one station wagon or van. You must also remember that there will be plenty of luggage to haul on the first and last days, even if you pack lightly. A single van will not carry seven or eight people and all their bags. Extra cars also allow for greater flexibility in your daily activities. One group might go hiking, another sightseeing to a small town, and another may just wish to stay in the villa with the occasional foray out for lunch or cappuccino.

Pool your money for food, wine and gas purchases into a "kitty" and do not allow it to be optional. Assure your group members that it is always cheaper to share expenses equally even if you have someone who claims to eat, drink, or use the car less than the others. It will not make much difference in the long run if one person eats cereal for breakfast and someone else eats eggs and toast. Non-drinkers can indulge in fancy fruit juices, which are as expensive as wine in Italy. Assign someone to be the "banker" and have each participant contribute about €100 at the start of the trip. Top it up as you go along and redistribute any leftover money at the end of your stay. Early on in your planning process, you should have a frank conversation about the type of food and wine you wish to purchase, and everyone should be in general agreement be it lavish, moderate, or modest. As a guideline, on a recent two week trip which I would characterize as modest, nine people each spent about €200 on food, wine and gas for the entire trip, including three restaurant lunches. That's only about €15 a day!

Hire a cleaning person once a week (included in some rentals, most provide it as an option) or designate one day a week as clean-up day and devote an hour or so to tidying the house. A large group of people can create a grimy mess over two weeks.

Take advantage of your kitchen and try to eat in the villa whenever possible. When I think back on past trips my fondest memories are of the meals that we cooked ourselves, and the pure sybaritic pleasure of sitting around the table sharing great food, wine, and conversation. Cooking together is not only much cheaper than eating out; it also creates a tremendous sense of conviviality. You can indulge in as much wine as you like without having to concern yourself with designating drivers or taking foolish risks. Shortly after you arrive at your rental, or even before you leave home, delegate cooking nights to the participants. The non-cooks in the group can make everyone happy with some salami and a roast chicken from a meat shop, a bagged salad from the supermarket and a loaf of bread from a bakery.

Try to assign bedrooms equitably. Bedrooms in large villas are usually not equal—there will often be a large master suite with an ensuite bathroom and a number of other bedrooms of various sizes that may or may not share bathrooms. First assign rooms to those with obvious requirements: the two singles travelling together will share the room with twin beds; the couple with the child will take the room with the double and the single; the person with the bad back can try all the beds to find the most comfortable; and the snorer can have the room at the end of the hall. Take whatever is left over and ask the remaining group members to draw lots. Sometimes one room will be clearly inferior and you may decide to switch half way through your stay. Make everyone understand, ideally before you leave on your vacation, that it is impossible to make the process completely fair and someone may get saddled with a less than perfect sleeping situation. If you have chosen your travelling mates carefully, most people will accept this with good grace.

Don't spend longer than two weeks with the same group. Personality quirks can change from endearing to annoying when you spend too much time together.

Don't allow for in and out privileges. You should make it clear to everyone that they will not be reimbursed for nights not spent in the villa — this applies to arriving late, leaving early or to short overnight jaunts to a different area.

Don't feel obligated to do everything together as a large group. Groups of people tend to get along better when they can spend their days following their own impulses and return to the villa in the evening with a good story to tell.

Travel with companions on a similar budget. It would be unwise for someone who is pinching pennies to travel with a person who thinks nothing of spending €50 on a bottle of wine and wants to eat all their meals in fancy restaurants.

Discuss your expectations beforehand and respect that we all have slightly different requirements for an ideal vacation. Is this trip about sheer relaxation, reading by the pool and catching up on much needed sleep? Or would you rather keep to a tight schedule of museum exhibitions, concerts and sightseeing? Is tasting at least 100 of the local wines a priority or are you content to drink the local plonk out of a jug? There is room for everyone in a large group, everyone that is except for those who are prone to complaining — they should be left behind!

"Good company in a journey makes the way to seem shorter."
ISAAK WALTON

Travelling with Children

I don't have children, but according to friends who do, Italy is one of the best places in the world to travel with kids. Despite the lowest birth rate in Europe, children are still treated like little *principi* and *principesse*. Restaurants will always welcome them and they will be cosseted and spoiled at every turn. Italian cities, particularly Rome, are the original "theme parks", and there are countless activities to keep your children occupied and thrilled. A vacation rental is the ideal accommodation—a garden will give them lots of room to run, play, and burn off excess energy, and with a kitchen you can cater to all of their peculiar food whims. If you choose to rent in a larger child-friendly complex in the summertime they will have plenty of young playmates, too.

Here is a website, an E-book and a guidebook to provide information to make your family trip memorable (and tolerable) for young and old members alike:

www.travelforkids.com has advice on travel essentials such as tips for eating out, packing, and travelling with stuffed animals, and a "fun things to do" section that covers most of the main tourist towns in Italy.

Kids Europe: Italy Discovery Journal
by P. L. Byrne
A downloadable book in PDF format available on Amazon.com, *Kids Europe* is a trip journal and guide with lots of fun activities to help give children an insight into Italian culture.

Italy with Kids
by Barbara Pape and Michael Calabrese, Open Road Publishing, 2003
Italy with Kids is considered the best all-round guide for families, with hotel and restaurant recommendations, suggestions for activities, and kid-friendly sightseeing.

కావ

Tools for Finding the Perfect Rental

How far in advance should I book?

If you want to get the best value for your money, don't delay in making a reservation. Everyone is looking for that special vacation rental with the perfect price/quality ratio and those rare places fill up quickly. Many villas designed for a group are reserved up to a year in advance, but nine months is usually sufficient time to give you a choice of great options. You can always find something (albeit not the best) three to six months out. If you have no choice but to book on short notice, try an agency—the larger ones will usually be able to come up with a couple of options and may have one or two last minute cancellations.

The Internet vs. catalogues

Whenever I try to convince my parents to buy a computer I am reminded that not everyone has embraced the computer age. The Internet has been my main resource for researching and booking rental properties in Italy for some years now. In fact, many agencies no longer publish catalogues due to the high cost of printing and postage. That said, there are few things more delightful than curling up in front of a fire on a cold winter evening with a stack of villa catalogues on your lap, happily indulging in fantasies of springtime in Tuscany. Of the rental agencies listed in this book, Parker Villas (pages 39-40) and Tuscan Enterprises (page 44) still offer catalogues as do these companies:

VACANCES PROVENÇALES VACATIONS
This Canadian company offers catalogues from the following agencies: Casa Club, Salogi, Home in Italy, and Cuendet. Order through their toll-free number or from their website.
1425 Bayview Avenue, Suite 204
Toronto, ON Canada, M4G 3A9
Toll-free: 800-263-7152
Phone: 416-322-5565
Fax: 416-322-0706
E-mail: rentals@europeanhomerentals.com
Web: www.europeanhomerentals.com

VILLE ET VILLAGE
Their Vacanze in Italia catalogue has over 400 listings and the Salogi
catalogue has a good selection of premium free-standing villas.
2124 Kittredge Street, #200
Berkeley, CA 94704 USA
Phone: 510-559-8080
Fax: 510-559-8217
E-mail: rentals@villeetvillage.com
Web: www.villeetvillage.com

ॐ

*"There is certainly no place in the world where a man may travel with greater
pleasure and advantage than in Italy. One finds something more particular in the
face of the country, and more astonishing in the works of nature than can be met
with any other part of Europe."*

JOSEPH ADDISON

The ideal website

Since I am making the assumption that most readers of this book will be
using the Internet to find their vacation home, here is a list of criteria I use
for judging a rental website. In a perfect world all of these elements would
be present, but at the very least, steer clear of sites with poor descriptions,
grainy photos and no listed prices.

Pictures, pictures and more pictures

It is easy to take a good photo or two, even in the worst hovel, but the
more pictures that are available, the easier it will be for you to examine
the property for what it really is. What can photographs tell you? Well,
they won't tell you the condition of the rental or the level of cleanliness,
but they will tell you the size of the dining room table, the configuration
of the living room and the number of comfortable chairs, the number of
windows (yes, there *are* windowless rentals!), the presence of lamps by
the bed, and the appearance of the surrounding countryside (although
there is nothing to stop an unscrupulous owner from taking that
splendid panorama shot from his best friend's living room window).
Just remember that the owner will always try to conceal the bad points:
the chain link fence that encircles the property, the busy road that runs
right past the house, or the neighbour's house that you can reach out
and touch from your bedroom window. Extra pictures are often
available to those who inquire.

Very specific descriptions

Compare the following descriptions for a typical four-person
apartment:

"Apartment for four people with one double size bedroom, main room
with double size bed, separate kitchenette, two bathrooms and private
entrance with direct access to the garden with spectacular view."

"Private entrance is into the dining room with fireplace and doors to the
various sections of the ground floor. On the right is the door that leads
into the sitting room. Another door leads into the fully equipped
kitchen with mixed range, electric oven and fridge, and a third door
opens into a spacious utilities room. In the dining room a flight of wood
steps leads to the upper floor open landing which offers a sitting area
and doors to the master bedroom, to the twin bedded room and to the
complete bathroom with bathtub. The house position is totally peaceful

and dominates the countryside in direction of Castellina in Chianti. It is very comfortably furnished with abundant use of solid wood pieces created by the owner who owns a small furniture company."

The first description reveals little—someone will have to sacrifice their privacy to sleep in the living room and the view is likely from the end of the garden, not from the windows in the house. In contrast, you could draw a floor plan from the second description. The kitchen equipment is listed, it tells you that there are two areas in which to sit and relax and that the house is quiet. Which apartment are you more likely to rent?

Beware of descriptors such as cozy (tiny) and rustic (uncomfortable furniture).

Honest descriptions

It is always in the agency's or owner's best interest to be upfront about any of the negative aspects of the unit. No property is perfect, and honesty instils the renter with a sense of confidence that there will be no hidden surprises. One of the agencies mentioned in this book, Parker Villas, always lists both the pluses and minuses of all their properties in their website descriptions.

Square footage

Why is it important to know the exact size if of a rental property? It will let you know if the property is the right size for your group. An apartment that sleeps four can range from 400 to over 1200 square feet, the former being perfect for a couple with a small child but likely too small for four adults. A 1200 square foot house would probably be unsuitable for eight adults even if it had four separate bedrooms. If this information isn't listed on the website, include it on your checklist of questions for the agency.

Floor plans

A floor plan can give you a lot of information. Do you have to walk through one bedroom to reach another? Is something described as a bedroom really just a bed on an open mezzanine? Is the one bathroom in a two-bedroom apartment an ensuite bathroom for the master bedroom? Owners can be reluctant to tell you about these little quirks, but they are common in many rental properties.

Prices

With today's technology there is no excuse for not including prices or at the very least, a price range. The absence of this information leads me to two conclusions: 1. The property is expensive and if I need to ask the price I probably can't afford it; 2. The owner is trying to hide something (which may or may not be the case—it just seems evasive to me). If I don't see prices, I simply move on.

On-line reviews

Many agencies now print on-line reviews. Even if some of the more negative comments have been edited (you should assume that this happens) you can still glean a lot of extra information about the property and the region from the experience of former renters.

Background information on the company

Look for the company's mission statement or philosophy, length of time in business, their criteria for choosing properties, payment and cancellation policies, and a telephone number and real physical address.

ॐॐ

"It must mean Italy.
Know'st thou the land where lemon-trees do bloom,
And oranges like gold in leafy gloom;
A gentle wind from deep blue heaven blows,
The myrtle thick, and high the laurel grows?
Know'st thou it, then?
Tis there! Tis there"

J. W. VON GOETHE

Large agencies, small agencies and renting from the owner

Your choice of rental agent can have a significant effect on the level of satisfaction that you have with your vacation rental. There are advantages and disadvantages to each, and I have pointed out the most obvious of these below. In the final analysis, it is up to you to decide which type of rental agent best meets your needs.

Large agencies

Advantages

- A large selection of rentals
- Represent properties in some of the less-travelled parts of Italy
- Alternate properties are usually available if problems arise
- Better for last-minute travel

Disadvantages

- Agents will be personally familiar with only a few properties
- Company may be representing a much larger Italian rental wholesaler, resulting in higher prices
- Properties may not be regularly inspected
- Company policy may emphasize quantity over quality

Small agencies

Advantages

- More personalized service
- Owner-operated — the person answering your e-mails is likely the boss
- Properties are hand selected and frequently inspected
- Agents know the properties and owners well
- Can be cheaper as the company deals directly with the owners

Disadvantages

- Lack of choice — small agencies represent a limited selection of properties
- Not great for last-minute travel — the good properties tend to book up early

Renting from the owner

Advantages

- ✎ A vast choice—the Internet has made it possible for owners to easily advertise their homes. Many property owners now prefer to rent directly to the public, keeping prices down and occupancy rates up.
- ✎ Lower prices—the owner does not pay an agency commission and the savings are passed on to the renter.

Disadvantages

- ✎ Unfortunately, this type of rental can be the most problematic as you are at the mercy of the owner if there are any difficulties. While the vast majority of landlords are trustworthy, there are sadly some unscrupulous operators out there.
- ✎ Standards can vary widely. The rental unit can show pride of ownership or it can be poorly maintained.

"The scene has an extraordinary charm. The air was almost solemnly still, and the large expanse of the landscape, with its gardenlike culture and nobleness of outline, its teeming valley and delicately-fretted hills, its peculiarly human-looking touches of habitation, lay there in splendid harmony and classic grace."

HENRY JAMES

Some popular agencies

The following are some of the more well-known players in the Italian vacation rental game — the field is vast and I encourage you to make your own discoveries but a glance through these listings will get you started on the road to finding your dream vacation home. Remember, using a reputable agency doesn't always guarantee you a good experience. You still have to do your homework and ask all the right questions about any of your potential choices.

Large agencies

ITALIANVILLAS.COM
Operating as an on-line agency since 1995, this enterprise has listings throughout Italy. The website is fantastic, with plenty of clear (read: not staged for the photo) pictures, prices, reviews (plus contact information for people who have stayed in the properties!) and on-line availability. One of the best features is their "Quick Pick" section that lists desirable properties in specific categories: "Really Interesting Places", "Our Best Values", "Places Great for Two People", "For Those Who Do Not Want to Rent a Car", etc. They have rentals in far-flung parts of the country like Pantelleria (an island off the coast of Sicily) and Sardinia. There are no real bargains here although the overall quality is high. They also arrange car rentals, private chefs and even truffle hunting in season.

Internet Villas Inc.
8 Knight Street, Suite 205
Norwalk, CT 06851 USA
Toll-free: 800-700-9549
Phone: 203-855-8161
Fax: 203-855-0506
E-mail: info@italianvillas.com
Web: www.italianvillas.com

PARKER VILLAS (THE PARKER COMPANY)
Parker Villas prides itself on its personalized service — after you have chosen a few potential rentals from their extensive selection of close to 300 villas and apartments they prefer to discuss and finalize your choice over the phone to insure you find something that really suits your needs. They have properties in Tuscany, Umbria, Venice and Rome as well as in areas

like Abruzzo, Puglia, Piemonte and Trentino. They offer multiple week discounts of up to 10% (for a three week rental) as well as a very interesting Rental Postponement Coverage which allows you to postpone your trip for any reason. The cost is 7% of the rental price and must be purchased at the time of booking—just the thing for a jittery 21st-century traveller. Their gorgeous catalogue *Undiscovered Italy* is available free to the United States and the United Kingdom (US$7 to Canada). Their website has on-line availability.

The Parker Company
Seaport Landing
152 Lynnway
Lynn, MA 01902 USA
Toll-free: 800-280-2811
Phone: 781-596-8282
Fax: 781-596-3125
E-mail: italy@theparkercompany.com
Web: www.theparkercompany.com or www.parkervillas.com

RENTVILLAS.COM
With over 1000 listings to choose from, Rentvillas.com represents one of Italy's largest and most well known vacation rental agencies, Cuendet. The website descriptions are detailed and the on-line reviews are very helpful—they are not afraid to print the negative comments to steer you away from the less than desirable properties (with this much product, not all of it can be good). This is the agency to turn to if you are looking for a rental in an off-the-beaten-path area like Puglia or Emilia Romagna. It also offers a good list of feature properties in many categories including "Island Escapes", "Rave Reviews", "Poolside Villas", and "Historic Castles" (note that these categories also include properties in other countries).

Rentvillas.com
700 E. Main Street
Ventura, CA 93001 USA
Toll Free: 800-726-6702
Phone: 805-641-1650
Fax: 805-641-1630
E-mail: mail@rentvillas.com
Web: www.rentvillas.com

Small agencies

DOMANI
This small agency, based in Washington State and run by Larry, Judy, Kathy and Scott Haase, has properties scattered across Italy with a good selection in Tuscany, Umbria and highly desirable Liguria. They also offer assistance with car and phone rental and hotel accommodation. They are an agent for the renowned Toscana Saporita cooking school. For music buffs they offer a tour to the Verona Opera festival each year.

Domani Inc.
3021 206th Way N.E.
Sammamish, WA 98074-4371 USA
Toll-free: 877-436-6264
Phone: 425-836-1017
Fax: 425-836-0487
E-mail: go.italy@domani-usa.com
Web: www.domani-usa.com

FLORENCE VILLAS
Australian Meaghan Barr runs this company, based in Lastra a Signa, just outside of Florence. The relatively small number of properties in Florence and throughout Tuscany allows Meaghan and her staff to keep an eye on quality. They offer extra cleaning services, arrange for in-villa cooking classes, and will even help to organize weddings and find student accommodation. The properties are generally good value for the money.

Florence Villas
Casella Postale 37
Signa, Florence, Italy 50058
Phone: +39 335 5845161
E-mail: info@florencevillas.net
Web: www.florencevillas.com

TUSCAN HOUSE

Tuscan House, a small agency based in Tuscany and the United States, has an informative website with gorgeous photos of property interiors and exteriors, on-line availability, as well as a list of recommended restaurants (all that I have tried have been superb). Most of the vacation homes are in Siena province in southern Tuscany, with a few properties in Lucca and Rome. This agency always garners rave reviews from former renters on the website www.slowtrav.com.

Tuscan House
Fax/voice mail: 801-640-5012
Reservations and requests: info@tuscanhouse.com
Web: www.tuscanhouse.com

Or contact:
Gulfstream Travel
P.O. Box 2049
Gulf Shores, AL 36547-2049 USA
Toll-free: 800-844-6939
Phone: 251-968-4444
Fax: 251-968-6191
E-mail: toptravel@aol.com

Note: During the winter months the owners of Tuscan House travel, and all inquiries should be sent by e-mail or fax—allow a few days for a reply.

UMBRIA RENTALS

Umbria Rentals is a tiny agency representing a handful of properties in or near one of my favourite small Umbrian towns, Panicale. In business since 1995, they offer both short and long-term rentals including the fabulous Rocca Buitoni, a small castle owned by the Buitoni pasta family. They also offer pottery and Italian classes.

Umbria Rentals
www.umbria-rentals.com
Contact through e-mail form on website

VIEWS ON VENICE

If you have ever fantasized about a few winter weeks in Venice without the crowds, this agency's multilingual staff will help you choose from a selection of well-furnished properties; from studios (starting at €800/week for two, an extremely reasonable price for one of the world's most expensive cities) all the way to glamorous apartments in important *palazzi*. The website is a bit cumbersome to use but the photos are excellent. They also allow you to rent for just three days at an increased per night fee.

Views on Venice
San Marco 4267/A
Venice, Italy
Phone: +39 041 2411149
Fax: +39 041 2415821
E-mail: info@viewsonvenice.com
Web: www.viewsonvenice.com

SUMMER IN ITALY

I prefer renting from a company that really knows their area of specialty. Summer in Italy is based in Salerno near most of their listings along the Amalfi and Sorrento coasts, in Cilento National Park, and on the island of Capri. Their website is terrific with lots of pictures, on-line availability, reviews and an excellent "Frequently Asked Questions" section for each property. This is a popular area and you are advised to book early. The prices are excellent, especially in the spring and fall.

Summer in Italy
Trotta Valentina
Viale delle Ginestre, 101
84134 Salerno Italy
Fax: +39 089 333438
E-mail: info@summerinitaly.com
Web: www.summerinitaly.com

TUSCAN ENTERPRISES
Charming Castellino in Chianti is the home of this medium-sized agency with over 200 properties, primarily in Tuscany. The website is not strong on pictures, but has superb detailed descriptions that include the square footage of each villa or unit, a feature I wish more companies would adopt. They have many multi-unit properties making it a good choice for couples or families (although a large group can save money by renting two apartments in lieu of one large house). A catalogue is available through their American representative, Villas D'Italia.

Villas d'Italia
962 Hobson Street
Walla Walla, WA 99362 USA
Phone: 509-526-4868
Fax: 509-529-7501
E-mail: info@villasditalia.com
Web: www.villasditalia.com
View Properties at www.tuscanenterprise.it

SUMMER'S LEASES
Summer's Leases, a company based in the U.K., has a hand-picked selection of over 60 properties, mostly in Umbria, with some in Tuscany and Rome. Their website could use a few more photographs but it has excellent descriptions and on-line availability. They respond to inquiries promptly and in great detail. One of the nice features of this company is that all payments are held in a trust account for your protection until you take your vacation. They also offer a one-week cooking course with housing in private apartments at Podere il Sapito, near San Gimignano.

Summer's Leases
66 West Common
Harpenden, Hertfordshire AL5 2LD England
Phone: (from UK) 0845 230 22 23
Phone: (from elsewhere) +44 1582 769952
E-mail: contact through form on website
Web: www.summersleases.com

IN TUSCANY
In operation since 1997, this company is run by Rebecca Taylor, an Australian who has made Tuscany her home. The agency has over 60 properties, all personally inspected by Rebecca. The excellent website has photos, floor plans, on-line availability and testimonials (undated). They also have a last-minute section that offers a discount on some of their properties booked between two weeks and one month in advance.

In Tuscany
Via Trieste, 89
53048 Sinalunga
Siena, Italy
Phone: +39 0577 630257
Fax: +39 0577 677618
E-mail: rebecca@intuscany.net
Web: www.intuscany.net

Rental-by-owner websites

VRBO—VACATION RENTALS BY OWNER
There are some very good values on this site with rental listings all over the world (you may get seduced by a beach villa in Bali). It is important to do careful research on these properties; they are not endorsed or inspected by the listing company. There are few pictures and no on-line reviews, but many listings have a link to the owner's website where you can find more complete information.
www.vrbo.com

HOLIDAY-RENTALS.COM
This site also offers worldwide rentals with hundreds in Italy. As in the previous entry, "buyer beware": Always make sure to get independent references for any property that you decide to rent.
www.holiday-rentals.co.uk

KNOWITAL.COM

Although not particularly well organized, Knowital.com has some very interesting and well-priced offerings. The site includes maps and background information on the various regions.

www.knowital.com

WORLDBY.COM

This group of sites under the umbrella of Worldby.com offers villas and apartments in addition to hotels and B&Bs. They are not an agency so you deal directly with the owners without having to pay a middleman. All prices I checked were the same as the owners' websites. The strength of these sites is in the photographs—most properties have at least twenty, including photos of bathrooms, kitchens, exteriors, and views of the surrounding countryside. A brand new search engine has made it easier to find a property based on accommodation type, area, price and amenities. The websites are especially good for hotels although it is a good idea to check **www.tripadvisor.com** or **www.venere.com** (page 93) for recent reviews.

www.italyby.com
www.florenceby.com
www.romeby.com
www.veniceby.com
www.tuscany.net

ॐ

The Search is On: Finding your Vacation Home

By now you have your travel dates picked out and have some idea of the kind of accommodation you will be renting (apartment or villa), where you will rent (city, town or countryside), your group's size and your specific destination. It is time to find your perfect vacation home; a rental that has what the Italians would call *un buon rapporto prezzo/qualità*—the best possible quality for the least amount of money. If you do not have access to the Internet I suggest you ask a friend or family member to help you with the search, otherwise you are limited to the few agencies that still print catalogues.

1. Begin by randomly searching the Internet to get an idea of the general range of prices for the type of home you are seeking. Give yourself plenty of time and don't be overwhelmed—think of this as the unofficial start of your vacation, your time to fantasize and plan to your heart's content. Start by inputting the name of the town, city or province nearest to your chosen rental area and follow it with "villa rental", "house rental" or "apartment rental", i.e. "Montepulciano apartment rental" or "Sicily villa rental". A search on the town, city or province plus "vacation rentals" will give you American sites. The same search on "holiday rentals" will give you websites in the United Kingdom. Bookmark the places that interest you.

2. Check out the agencies listed in this book to compare prices and descriptions with what you have found searching randomly. Bookmark the properties that fill your requirements.

3. You now need to narrow your choices and pick the five or six properties that come closest to meeting your needs. If you are thinking of renting through an agency, you should have a second and third choice as fallback if the first isn't available.

4. Now you want to see if you can find a better price for these properties somewhere else on the Internet. The logic is this: Very few owners will have an exclusive agreement with one agency. Most will list their property with a few agencies and then list it on a rental-by-owner site or their personal website. A listing on an agency website tells you one important thing: at one time an independent person who was not the owner inspected the property and deemed it suitable for their clients. This means that it exhibits

at least a minimum level of cleanliness and good management. Your job as a smart traveller is to try to find a better price for this property through another agency or the owner's website. This is *not* to say that you shouldn't use agencies, in fact, I use them most of the time. You should consider rental agencies and the extra money you spend on renting a property through them a kind of traveller's insurance—if something goes wrong with the unit that can't be remedied you always have some recourse—they can find you a different apartment, or give you a partial or full refund. This is not always the case when you deal directly with the owner. On the other hand, it is not fair for agencies to charge unreasonable mark-ups (sometimes up to €1500 per week above the owner's price). Unless they are offering substantially more than what the owner or another agency includes in the price (like daily maid service, a telephone, and all heating or air conditioning) you should consider the lower priced option.

Finding a better deal can be a little tricky. Agencies will likely change the description slightly (in most cases the property name) to keep you from tracking it down in another location. First do a search using the property name and the geographical location. If that doesn't work, look for a characteristic in the property description that makes it unique and do a search on that, along with the location and "apartment rental" or "villa rental". For example: Let's say that the apartment you have found is near the Accademia gallery in Florence and has two bedrooms and a terrace. Try inputting "Florence apartment rental, two bedrooms, terrace, Accademia Gallery" and see what comes up. Keep in mind that some agencies have exclusive listings and you will not be able to find them cheaper elsewhere— the important thing is that the price is within your budget—I wouldn't worry about saving a few extra euros if the property suits you perfectly.

5. Try to find more information about your choices. Read on-line reviews, if available, and visit **www.slowtrav.com**, the informative website of Slow Travel, an on-line organization that promotes vacation rentals as an alternative to "travelling in the fast lane". Members can post reviews of places they have recently rented but there is no need to register to read the reviews. I would take any review older than two years with a grain of salt. Rental properties take a lot of wear and tear over time and a once pristine apartment can quickly become shabby if a regular regimen of cleaning and maintenance is not followed. Reviews are no substitute for references.

6. Narrow your choices down to two or three and make contact with the agencies or owners. First, ask if the property is available for your chosen dates. It pays to be flexible—taking a holiday a week later or a week earlier can mean the difference between your first and second choice. Use the checklist on pages 51 and 52 and ask any questions that are not covered in the website or catalogue description. Ask for a reference if you are not satisfied with the on-line reviews that you have found. This should not be a copy of a letter they send you as an attachment but an e-mail address or phone number for a person who has actually stayed there.

7. Now that you have all your information you can make your decision. Ask the owners or agencies to hold your choices for a few days while you consult with your travelling companions to make the final decision. Pay the deposit and start saving your money for the vacation of a lifetime.

Hunting for a vacation rental is like hunting for a house to purchase—the more you look, the more you get an indication of the bigger picture: general price ranges in various areas and the kinds of features you can actually get for the money. Don't rent the first place you find—take some time to really look around and get a picture of the whole rental landscape.

How do I find a cheaper rental?

Rent in the off-season. Prices usually drop near the beginning of October and increase again between the end of April and the middle of May. Keep in mind that if you rent in early spring, late autumn or winter there may be heating costs involved. Try to find a rental that includes heat.

Find a rental without a swimming pool. Pools are very expensive to heat and maintain. Unless you rent in mid-summer a pool is by no means a necessity.

Skip the luxuries. Most North Americans expect to find dishwashers, American refrigerators, big fancy kitchens and ensuite bathrooms in a vacation rental. If you are willing to live more like the locals and forgo a few of the extras you will be able to find cheaper options. *Agriturismi*, or farms that rent apartments, are often good sources for simpler and less expensive accommodation. The website **www.agriturismo.com** has hundreds of listings and allows you to contact the owners directly.

Make a last-minute booking. With the uncertainty that the last few years have brought to the travel industry it has been possible to get discounts on last-minute cancellations and unrented properties. I don't really recommend this unless you have decided to take a vacation on the spur of the moment. You could find yourself completely out of luck or staying in sub-standard accommodation.

Avoid the popular areas. Don't rent in Rome, Venice or Florence and if you have your heart set on Tuscany, avoid Chianti, or consider renting in Umbria, Le Marche, or Northern Lazio instead — these areas are just as pretty and much cheaper.

When travelling with a group rent two or three smaller apartments instead of one large villa. Some multi-unit complexes have a common room where everyone can gather and often one of the apartments will have a table large enough for the whole group (or you can make arrangements with the owner to have an extra table brought in).

Rent directly from the owner. Covered in the previous section.

ॐॐ

The essential questions: A renter's checklist

The following checklist includes most of the items that are important to know about any potential rental before you sign on and pay your deposit. Read through the website or catalogue description, study the photos, and check off any of the following questions that are not answered. The resulting list will cover most of what you need to ask the agency when you contact them. This doesn't mean that a rental *must* have screens, a dishwasher or an oven to be acceptable—it just allows you to make an informed choice and avoid surprises on arrival. The first checklist contains all of the mandatory questions; the second has optional items. Only inquire about what is really important to you—a rental is a two-way transaction and if the owner thinks you may be a "high maintenance" tenant, they may choose not to rent to you.

Mandatory questions

- ☐ Where is the rental located?
- ☐ Is the property an apartment or a stand-alone house?
- ☐ How many apartments or villas are in the complex?
- ☐ Is the owner or caretaker on site or nearby?
- ☐ How close are the neighbours?
- ☐ How close is the rental to a major road?
- ☐ What is the size of the rental unit in square feet/metres?
- ☐ How far is the nearest bar/grocery store/town?
- ☐ Does the property have a telephone? Is cell phone rental available?
- ☐ Do I need a car?
- ☐ How many parking spaces are there?
- ☐ Is there a terrace? Is it furnished?
- ☐ Is the house/apartment bright and sunny?
- ☐ How many bedrooms are there? Singles, doubles, triples?
- ☐ What is the total number of beds and the maximum number of guests?
- ☐ How many bathrooms are there? How many toilets, baths and showers?
- ☐ Are all of the bedrooms separate and individual (not pass through)?
- ☐ Are the bathrooms ensuite or communal?
- ☐ Do the windows have screens?
- ☐ How many people does the dining room table seat?
- ☐ How many people does the living room seat comfortably?
- ☐ Are the linens included? How often are they changed?
- ☐ Is there an oven?
- ☐ Is there a dishwasher?

- ☐ Is there a washing machine?
- ☐ Are electricity, gas and water included in the price?
- ☐ What is the cost per week?
- ☐ How much is the deposit?
- ☐ When is the balance due?
- ☐ How much is the damage deposit?
- ☐ Is final cleaning included in the rental price?
- ☐ Is extra cleaning available?
- ☐ Do you offer discounts for multi-week rentals?
- ☐ What is your cancellation policy?
- ☐ What are the terms of payment? (credit card, money order, bank draft, cash)

Optional questions

- ☐ Is the property suitable for children/the elderly/the disabled?
- ☐ Do you accept pets?
- ☐ Is there air conditioning/heating and is it included in the price?
- ☐ Is there a barbecue?
- ☐ Do you have bicycles available to rent?
- ☐ Is there a golf course/horseback riding/tennis nearby?
- ☐ Is there a comfortable sofa?
- ☐ Is a floor plan available?
- ☐ How old is the building?
- ☐ How is the house furnished? (rustic, comfortable, elegant)
- ☐ Does the caretaker or agency representative speak English?
- ☐ Do you have a list of recommended restaurants?
- ☐ Is there a swimming pool? Is it shared?
- ☐ Is there a television/VCR/CD player?
- ☐ Does the property have nice views?
- ☐ Is a cook available for hire?
- ☐ Is there a hair dryer?
- ☐ Is the house equipped with a crib and a high chair?
- ☐ Are the beds equipped with orthopaedic mattresses?
- ☐ Is smoking permitted in the house?

The Renter's Responsibilities

- ❧ Treat the property as if it were your own—use coasters under drinks on wooden surfaces, don't leave dirty dishes in the sink overnight as an enticement to furry and flying critters, and keep the house generally tidy.

- ❧ If you rearrange any of the furniture, return it to its original position before you leave.

- ❧ Always turn out lights that you are not using. Turn off all lights, close the shutters, and lock the door before you leave for the day.

- ❧ Keep stereo and television noise at a reasonable level, particularly if you are staying in a multi-unit property. Also be aware that sound travels at night and you should keep your voices down if you like to spend late evenings on the terrace or balcony.

- ❧ Report all breakage and any damage.

- ❧ Before you call the owner with a problem, try to solve it yourself. Learn the location of the fuse box and instructions for all the household appliances when you arrive. The owner or caretaker will be happy to help you with any issues that may arise but keep in mind that they are not a concierge.

Car Rental

U nless you are staying in a large city or town with good public transportation you will require a car. Forget what everyone has told you about Italians behind the wheel—they drive fast, but they take their driving seriously and are excellent defensive drivers.

Renting a car after you arrive in Italy is expensive; you will save as much as 50% on the rental price if you organize your rental car before you leave home. All of the major car rental companies are represented in Italy, but you can save time by renting through Auto Europe, **www.autoeurope.com**, an on-line rental consolidator. They consistently have the best rates, which include all insurance and most taxes. If you find a better price elsewhere they will try to match it.

In Italy, standard transmissions are the norm. If you are not comfortable driving a standard, a couple of lessons before you leave home will increase your confidence. Do *not* try to learn in Italy—ask someone else to drive or rent a car with an automatic transmission (at a substantial premium, unfortunately).

While driving in the Italian countryside can be exhilarating, most people find driving in the city terrifying. The best solution is to either pick up your car at the airport or in a smaller town accessible via the main rail line near your property rental. For example, Chiusi—a small town mid-way between Rome and Florence—has a car rental office across the street from the train station and is a good starting point for anywhere in Northern Lazio, Southern Tuscany or Umbria. Under any circumstance you will appreciate the relative ease of driving out of a small town, but all the more so if you are bleary-eyed and suffering from jet lag.

Gas

The price of gas (*benzina*) in Italy will shock you; remember that cars are smaller and more efficient and distances are shorter—you probably won't spend much more on gas than you do at home. Before you leave the car rental agency find out whether the car takes unleaded gas (*senza piombo*) or diesel—the wrong gas can destroy the engine. Also assure that you have a full tank of gas and remember to fill up before you return the car.

International Driver's Licence

An International Driver's Licence is a requirement to drive in Italy. Car rental agencies will not request it for the rental contract (but will ask for a driver's licence from your home country), but the police will expect you to have one if you are ever pulled over. They are easily obtainable at any branch of your local automobile association for a small fee. You do not have to take a road test, but they should supply you with a brochure with some tips on driving and pictures of the local signage.

Some tips for surviving the driving

Use the passing lane on a four-lane highway only for passing. Unlike North America where meandering along aimlessly in either lane has become the norm, Italians will express their strong disapproval if you are foolish enough to use the passing lane for regular travel. Expect them to flash their headlights, blast the horn or drive within an inch or two of your bumper. When you wish to pass, signal your lane change and move into the passing lane. Return quickly to the slow lane once you have completed the pass.

Always shoulder check before changing lanes. Europeans drive very fast and cars can appear out of nowhere, even after you have checked your rear and side mirrors.

Avoid driving in big cities unless you have some kind of a death wish (or at least a dent wish). Big cities are chaotic, with their one-way streets, darting motorbikes and aggressive drivers. If you are travelling to the city for a day from a villa in the country it is a good idea to park your car in a small town along a train line and take the train into town.

Drive with a good navigator. Roads are generally well marked, but an extra set of eyes and a good map will insure you get to your destination with relatively few unplanned side-trips.

Don't drive into small villages. Narrow village roads are passable only with the smallest of cars and are often off-limits to all but residents or delivery people. There are generally large parking lots outside of small towns; some are free and some have meters or parking attendants.

Buy a good map. The best are put out by the *Touring Club Italiano* and are available in North America and Italy. **But don't become a slave to your map.** Among the pleasures of driving in Italy are the amazing discoveries you make by taking shortcuts and getting completely lost.

Don't drink and drive. Somehow we all feel invulnerable on vacation but tourists *are* killed on Italy's roads as a result of alcohol. Know your own limits and always have a designated driver if you are planning a big wine-soaked lunch or dinner out.

Watch out for cyclists. On weekends country roads are full of cycling clubs out for exercise and friendly competition. Be wary, too, of elderly farmers weaving precariously along the roadside on grocery-laden bicycles.

Car sickness

The narrow winding country roads in Italy can challenge the strongest stomachs. If you suffer from motion sickness, sit in the front seat and look straight ahead. Those with more severe queasiness should carry a supply of anti-nausea medication or try an effective product called Sea-bands, a cloth bracelet embedded with a small plastic ball that stimulates an acupuncture point and prevents motion sickness without the drowsy side effects of medication. They are available at pharmacies or on line at **www.sea-band.com**.

Packing

There is no point trying to keep up with the Italians when it comes to fashion. *La bella figura,* the art of looking good, is almost a national spectator sport and many Italians follow fashion trends slavishly. Keep your clothing simple—for practicality I stick to a palette of dark neutrals with a few bright accents in my tops and accessories. Dress for comfort but know that nothing will brand you more as a tourist than white sneakers, shorts, a logo T-shirt and a waist pack for your valuables.

The most seasoned travellers pack lightly, and I encourage you to do so as well. Some people I know take minimal clothing and use it as an excuse to shop for a new wardrobe. Even if you are going to stay in one place for several weeks, you still have to get there, and heaving an enormous suitcase on and off trains, in and out of taxis, and finally into the tiny trunk of your Italian rental car outweighs what little advantage might come from hauling those extra but unnecessary items with you. As far as clothing is concerned, most rentals have a washing machine either in the unit or a shared facility somewhere on the property. At the very least they will be able to direct you to a place in town where you can have your laundry done. Travelling home is a different matter though—I can put up with the added weight when I know that my extra bag is filled with wine, olive oil, fabulous linens, pasta and other assorted goodies that I have picked up on my trip. I travel with a 20-inch expandable rolling carry-on for anything up to a month. (I can't always carry it on though—it often exceeds the airline's weight limit for carry-on.) Tucked inside are a small daypack and a folding nylon bag.

For more information and tips on packing there is an excellent website called **www.travelite.org** where you will find recommendations on buying luggage, information on wardrobe selection, packing methods, and packing lists.

Here is a sample packing list for a spring or fall trip to Tuscany (you may need a heavier sweater further north). This list assumes that you will do your laundry once a week and wash a few undergarments in the sink.

Women's packing list

1 pair lightweight jeans or black cotton pants
1 pair black cotton pants
1 pair khaki cotton pants
1 pair dress-up black pants or skirt
1 lightweight cardigan
1 lightweight sweater set (the cardigan can be worn with other things)
2 long-sleeve cotton shirts
3 long-sleeve T-shirts
4 short-sleeve T-shirts
1 dressy top
1 pair light cotton pyjamas
1 large light wool or cashmere shawl (great for staying warm on the plane)
1 cotton scarf
1 pair dark walking shoes
1 pair black (slightly dressier) walking shoes
1 pair dress-up shoes
Thigh-length microfiber jacket
Bathing suit
5 bras
5 panties
5 pairs socks
Light house slippers
Ultra-light umbrella

Men's packing list

1 pair jeans
1 pair good quality black pants
1 pair cotton khaki or black pants
4 good quality T-shirts
1 long-sleeve T-shirt
2 long-sleeve shirts with collar
1 light wool sweater
1 sports jacket (optional)
Microfiber rain jacket
5 pairs underwear

5 pairs socks
1 pair swimming trunks
1 pair sneakers
1 pair black walking shoes
1 pair sandals or house slippers
Light cotton robe or pyjamas

Optional for hikers

1 pair hiking pants with zip-off legs
1 pair hiking boots
2 pairs hiking socks
Sun hat

Other useful items

Travel alarm clock
A flashlight, book light or headlamp for night time reading and
    emergencies
English language books
Guidebooks and a phrasebook
A few CDs (if the property has a music system)
Pool towel (if required)
Earplugs (for snoring companions and early morning roosters)
Folding nylon bag
Deck of playing cards

And don't forget: Passport, credit and debit cards, driver's licence and
International Driver's Licence, tickets, car rental contract and location of car
rental agency, directions to the rental property and relevant telephone
numbers, travel insurance and medical coverage card, prescription and
over-the-counter medication, sunglasses, spare eyeglasses or contact lenses,
camera, address book, photocopies of your passport and credit cards, and
plenty of euros!

৵৹

Arriving at your Rental

Most properties are rented for a full week, usually from Saturday to Saturday, and you will be asked to arrive either in the late afternoon or early evening. You are now faced with a dilemma: Most car rental offices close for the weekend at 1 p.m. on Saturday, leaving a gap of several hours between picking up the car and arriving at the rental, fine if you have a long drive ahead of you, but if the villa is nearby you will be tempted to leave your car unattended with all of the luggage in the trunk while you go shopping or sightseeing. *Please do not do this!* Ask the villa owner or agent if you can drop your luggage off early and return later to check in or have someone wait with the car while you shop. Theft from cars is common, even in the most unlikely places. We have never left anything in our rental cars but have found the trunk forced open by would-be thieves on more than one occasion.

If your flight arrives in the late afternoon and you are considering driving to your villa in the countryside the same evening, I would advise you to find a hotel for the night and set out the following morning. Many country villas are difficult enough to find in broad daylight; driving aimlessly and lost on a narrow gravel road in the dark is frustrating and potentially dangerous.

The check-in

The owner or representative will be waiting at the vacation home when you arrive and you should familiarize yourself with the workings of the rental unit while they are still there to answer your questions. You will be asked for a damage deposit based on the terms of your rental agreement. If you pay the deposit in cash, ask for a receipt. You should get as much information as possible, but you will certainly need to know the following:

- **Instructions for the washing machine.** Ask for a quick tutorial on the operation of the front-loading washing machine—they are not self-explanatory and the instruction manual will be in Italian. They generally take longer than an hour to wash your clothes but do an excellent job. I have yet to see a dryer in Italy—check with the rep to make sure that you have a clothesline or drying rack.

- **Instructions for the stove and oven.** You may need a match or a flint to light these.

- **Location of the electrical fuse box.** You will invariably blow a fuse at some time during your stay and you don't want to have to call someone to help if all you need to do is simply throw a switch.

- **Instructions for disposal of garbage and recycling.** There is no household garbage pick-up in Italy. The agent will direct you to the nearest public trash and recycling receptacles found along the roadside.

- **Instructions for the dishwasher.** Most European dishwashers require a water softening salt along with the detergent.

- **Instructions for heating and air conditioning.** If they are not included in the rental price remember to use them prudently as they can be very expensive.

- **Demonstration of satellite TV, video player and stereo.**

- **Location and hours of nearest shops and restaurants and information about local events.**

- **Emergency contact number.**

- **General villa walk-through.** Take note of any previous damage to furniture or appliances.

ॐॐ

If you are travelling with a group it is advisable to hide a spare house key somewhere on the property, and make sure that everyone knows where it is.

Check the cupboards and make a shopping list

Most rentals will provide you with a few rolls of toilet paper, a couple of extra garbage bags, salt and pepper, and not much else. You need to look through the cupboards and make a shopping list based on what you find. Sometimes a few ingredients like sugar or olive oil will be left over from the previous tenant but many owners will remove everything after each rental period. You should also check to make sure that you have a coffee maker or *moka*, a pasta pot and a cheese grater (the essentials for life in Italy).

On your first shopping trip stock up with staples and any ingredients you will need until Monday morning (most shops are closed on Sunday), and pick up a few convenience foods for a simple meal or snack.

A sample shopping list

Sugar
Olive oil
Vinegar (red wine or regular balsamic)
Coffee and tea
Milk (low fat milk is called *parzialmente scremato*)
Cream
Bread
Breakfast cereal
Butter
Eggs
Jam
Fresh pasta
A few packages of dried pasta
A few jars of *passata di pomodoro* (tomato purée)
Onions
Garlic
Carrots
Celery
Fresh parsley
Fresh basil
A small tub of freshly prepared pesto
Salad ingredients
Crackers
Fruit juice
Assorted cheeses including a chunk of Parmigiano-Reggiano, some
    Gorgonzola, and a tub each of mascarpone and ricotta

Assorted proscuitto and salami
Dried beans or lentils
Bouillon cubes (*dadi di brodo*)
Fresh fruit
Ingredients (fruit, vegetables and meat) for any planned dishes
Bottled water (fizzy and still)
Wine
Toilet paper
Matches or lighter
Garbage bags
Paper towels
Paper napkins (or buy cloth napkins at a shop or market)
Dish soap
Bar soap
Dishwashing detergent
Laundry detergent
Plastic wrap or aluminum foil
Candles

Here are examples of some quick and easy meals that you can make with the ingredients on hand to keep you going until Monday:

BREAKFAST: Bread and butter with jam; bread with mascarpone or ricotta and jam; scrambled eggs with toast; frittata made with vegetables, eggs and Parmesan cheese; cereal and milk.

LUNCH AND DINNER: Bruschetta with tomatoes, garlic and basil; soup made with lentils, carrots, celery and onions, a few spoonfuls of *passata* and a stock cube, topped with pesto; spaghetti with a sauce made from heating some gorgonzola cheese with a little fresh cream; grilled proscuitto and cheese sandwiches; tomato *passata* cooked with proscuitto or pancetta, onions, garlic and basil, poured over pasta; spaghetti tossed with pesto and mascarpone cheese.

One of the challenges for North Americans is getting used to Italian shopping hours. Most shops, including supermarkets, are closed on Sunday and often one other day a week. They also close for a lunch break from 1 to 4 p.m. Plan accordingly.

Restaurants vs. Cooking for Yourself

Italy is a food lover's dream. From the simple, almost ascetic cuisine of Tuscany and Umbria to the more complex creations of Emilia Romagna and Piemonte, Italy brings out the glutton in everyone.

The most important thing to know about reasonably priced restaurants in any particular region of Italy is this—they all serve pretty much the same thing. If you are in Rome, virtually every trattoria will have a version of *cacio e pepe*, pasta with Pecorino Romano cheese and black pepper. If you stay near Montepulciano you will become familiar with *pici al cinghiale*, hand-rolled spaghetti with wild boar sauce. Italians don't go out to dinner so much to be dazzled with innovation, but to socialize with friends and eat the dishes that are the known specialties of the region. That is not to say that these restaurants aren't wonderful—in fact I prefer this type of food: simple, with distinct straightforward flavours, and eaten in the context of the local wines and local terrain. Most Italians would agree with me when I say that the best food to be had is in private homes, particularly if there is a grandmother behind the stove. That is precisely what makes cooking at your rented villa so exciting. Armed with a good cookbook, some excellent fresh ingredients and a bit of imagination you can create unforgettable meals. Don't expect a huge variety of produce though, as Italians still eat by the seasons, so your choices will be limited to what is available locally (or at least in Western Europe) with a few imports thrown into the mix for interest.

But who would travel to Italy and not want to try the fabulous restaurants? Here are some suggestions and tips for:

Dining out in Italian restaurants

Reservations

Whenever possible make a reservation—popular establishments and restaurants with only a handful of tables will absolutely require one. In an Italian restaurant the table is yours for the evening; a reservation allows the chef to plan food purchases. In the quiet season some restaurants in the countryside will not even bother to open if they don't have any bookings.

Meal times

Lunch or *il pranzo* is usually served from about 12:30 to 2 p.m., although most people don't start until 1. Dinner or *la cena* is normally from 7 or 7:30 p.m. until 9:30 or 10 p.m. In the countryside people tend to eat dinner a little earlier starting at 7:30 or 8, but if you choose to eat at 7:30 in a larger city like Rome or Florence you will find yourself surrounded by other tourists—urban Italians don't start dinner until 9.

The Italian restaurant meal

An Italian meal is comprised of a series of courses, normally eaten in a specific order:

Antipasti

Literally "before the meal", the antipasto is a small course often consisting of sliced meats, *bruschette* or *crostini*, some kind of a fritter (like fried zucchini blossoms) or an assortment of vegetables. It should just stimulate your appetite for the dishes to come, not kill it. In a fancier restaurant the antipasto may be a more composed, elegant plate, but usually it is quite rustic and served without undue ceremony.

Primi

Pasta is generally not considered the main meal in Italy and is almost always served as a first course or *primo* (although you may choose to have it as your main course if you wish—more about that later). Other common *primi* are risotto, gnocchi, or soup. The portions are usually small enough to combine with a main course, but if you wish you can sometimes split one portion between two persons—a half order often comes with a surcharge.

Secondi

The *secondo* or second course is what North Americans would think of as the main course, although in Italy it is meant to be a complement to the first course. Food is not served in the walloping portions that have become common in North America, and vegetable accompaniments or *contorni* are ordered separately. This course will include grilled, braised, or roasted meat, poultry or fish, often served very simply with olive oil and lemon. Chic restaurants will serve more elaborate dishes.

Contorni

Contorni are side dishes: salads, roasted or French-fried potatoes, braised beans, grilled vegetables and the like. Vegetarians can often make a very nice meal of a vegetarian pasta dish and a few *contorni* served as the main course.

Dolci

Toothsome cakes, pastries and confections abound in Italy, but they tend to be served on their own as a late morning or afternoon snack, not after a heavy noon or evening meal. At home people often just have a piece of fresh fruit for dessert and in a very simple trattoria this may be your only choice. Tiramisu is ubiquitous in Italy and most trattorias offer a version of this dessert. There is also likely to be a freshly baked cake, a custard tart, or some biscotti to dip in sweet wine.

Pane

Bread is always served with your meal and the quality can range from house-made specialty bread to the rather diabolical unsalted bread of Tuscany. Butter is not served with bread—try eating it as Italians do, as a complement to the food, not as something to fill up on while you wait for your meal to arrive. It is not considered rude to mop up the delicious juices remaining on your plate with your bread, but in a more upscale restaurant you may want to spear the bread chunk with a fork to get the job done.

The Italian government is trying to phase out the *pane e coperto*, a charge (a euro or two per person) for bread and tablecloth washing, but you may still find it on your bill in certain restaurants. It is not the same as the *servizio*, or service charge.

Acqua

While tap water in Italy is perfectly safe to drink, bottled water is the norm in restaurants. Your waiter will ask if you would like *acqua frizzante* (with gas—you can also say *con gas*) or *acqua naturale* (still water).

Vino

Wine prices in shops and supermarkets are reasonable; wine in restaurants is expensive. If you are trying to save money, stick to the house wine, the *vino della casa*. Look around to see if the other patrons are drinking it and ask for a small taste if you are unsure—some house wines are virtually undrinkable.

Ordering in an Italian restaurant

On my first few trips to Italy I always left restaurants feeling uncomfortably full. I had read in guidebooks that it was imperative to order all or at least most of the courses on the menu or risk incurring the wrath of the wait staff and the kitchen. Then I began to notice Italians stopping into a trattoria for lunch having nothing more than a plate of pasta and a small bottle of water or patrons at dinner having an antipasto followed by pasta, salad and dessert and passing on the second course altogether. It is a common fallacy that you must order all of the courses in a restaurant and limit light lunches to a quick *panino* in a bar. Italians have also become health conscious of late and it is no coincidence that obesity is not one of the country's main concerns.

I would encourage you, however, to order at least three courses when you go out to a restaurant or trattoria in the evening. Profit margins in the restaurant business are slim and the table you reserve is yours for the evening — the restaurant will not be able to make up the lost income on another table if you consume nothing more than a plate of pasta and a salad. Finer restaurants will expect you to order at the very least a *primo*, *secondo*, and a dessert. Remember that a salad is never a meal unless the restaurant specializes in *insalatone* or "big salads".

Also be aware that the restaurant chef is not your private chef. In North America we have become accustomed to asking restaurants to accommo-date our dining idiosyncrasies: low-carb and low-fat diets, strange food combinations, and unusual likes and dislikes. While most restaurants can assist vegetarians and those with specific allergies, the attitude in Italy is this: If you didn't want to eat what was offered on the menu, a selection of the chef's freshest and finest, why on earth would you be here in the first place?

Changing the order of courses in a restaurant meal *is* possible, if you make your intentions clear to your server. For example if you would like to start you meal with spaghetti with clams and follow it with two *contorni* , spinach and braised beans, you would say, "*Come primo, vorrei spaghetti vongole; come secondo, vorrei spinaci e fagioli in umido*". The server may raise his eyebrows slightly but will understand what you mean.

The interminable wait for *il conto*

When you have finished your meal and are ready to leave you will request the cheque, "*Il conto, per favore*". Prepare yourself for one of the oddest waiting games imaginable. You will wait, and wait, and wait some more. Perhaps it is because most bills are still hand-written and restaurants are minimally staffed—servers need to wait until the end of service to find the time to write up the bill. Or maybe they feel they are rushing you by giving you the cheque before the very end of the evening. Don't worry, the cheque will arrive.

Tipping

One of the biggest mysteries to me about dining in Italy is tipping. Every guidebook that I've read offers different advice. Some say leave nothing if the service is included and 10% if it is not. Others say that you should always leave a little extra even if the service charge is included. The owner of a Florentine hotel once told me that you should leave about 10%, even if the service is included because it is usually the restaurant owner and not the server who receives the service charge. Confused yet? I cannot tell you what to do but I will tell you what *I* do: I leave about 10% for good service, always in cash, even if the service is included, particularly if the server appears to be an employee and not the owner. Some people tell me that Italians don't tip very much and that tipping generously makes me look like a silly foreigner, but I've worked in restaurants, I know how difficult it is, and when I get good service I want to reward the server—I can live with the label.

"An Italian meal is a story told from nature, taking its rhythms, its humors, its bounty and turning them into episodes for the senses."
MARCELLA HAZAN

When in Rome...the etiquette of eating in Italy

Italian cuisine is rooted in hundreds of years of tradition and Italians tend to be less free-wheeling in their eating habits. There are some fairly hard and fast rules that you should be aware of—this doesn't mean that you can't break them, you are the customer after all—it will just help to explain the widened eyes, raised eyebrows and occasional outright refusal from the server when you make, what is to them, a strange request.

- We may consider pasta naked without the requisite sprinkle of Parmesan cheese, but in Italy it is never added to any sauce containing fish or shellfish.

- Italians do not use a spoon for twirling their long pasta. Simply capture a few strands in the tines of your fork and twirl them on the side of your plate.

- Balsamic vinegar or at least *aceto balsamico tradizionale* is a very special condiment, drunk after a meal as a digestive or drizzled on roasted meat or chicken. The commercial style balsamic vinegar that is used as an all-purpose vinegar in North America is not as popular in Italy (although it is available in every supermarket). The vinegar on your restaurant table will be red or white wine vinegar.

- You will never be offered a small dish with a mixture of oil and balsamic vinegar for dipping bread. This is an Italian-American restaurant invention.

- Pepper is considered a spice that complements some foods and not others and is not sprinkled over everything. If the waiter thinks that fresh pepper goes with the dish you have ordered the grinder will be offered. You will also notice the absence of a saltshaker on the table. In my experience, food in Italy is more likely to be over- than under-salted, but feel free to ask for salt (*sale*) if you require it.

- Cappuccino and *caffelatte* are morning drinks, generally not consumed after about 11 a.m. Coffee ordered after a meal is always espresso, but if the restaurant has the proper equipment they will be happy to make a cappuccino for you. Decaffeinated coffee is available—ask for *decaffeinato*.

ೋೋ

Food Shopping and Cooking in Italy

For me, having a kitchen at my disposal and the ability to shop at local markets is the stuff that dreams are made of. But even if time spent near the stove is your idea of a holiday in hell, shopping for yourself and preparing even the simplest of meals can save you money and provide you with some of the warmest memories of your vacation in Italy. While shopping you have contact with the locals and plenty of opportunity for cultural exchange as well as the prospect of making some hilarious gaffes that permit you to laugh at yourself (don't ask how I know). Don't try to cook what you cook at home—leave your diet behind, buy yourself a good Italian cookbook and gear your meals to what is available in your area.

Food shops

In the past, shopping in Italy meant trips to a series of small shops, each specializing in a specific kind of food product. This is still a great option and in fact your only alternative in some places. The etiquette for shopping doesn't vary much from store to store. The proprietor is there to assist you and attends to customers in the order in which they enter the store. Do not interrupt the salesperson while they are helping another customer, simply wait your turn—they will give you their undivided attention once the previous customers have been served. Indicate what you would like to purchase by pointing to the item, rather than picking it up yourself.

Here is a list of the small shops you will find in your travels:

Macelleria or Butcher Shop
Not just a butcher per se, a *macelleria* will often sell cured pork products and prepared dishes like roasted chicken and potatoes.

Salumeria or Pork Butcher's Shop
These shops specialize in all kinds of cured pork products.

Alimentari or Grocery Store
Alimentari carry a little bit of everything including cheese, cured meats, produce, and dry goods.

Panificio or Bread Bakery
Usually limited to various kinds of bread.

Forno or "Oven"
Also a bakery, selling bread and pastry.

Pasticceria or Pastry Shop
Pasticcerie are often equipped with tables and chairs and serve coffee, drinks and light lunches along with the delicious pastry.

Frutta e Verdura or Fruit and Vegetable Shop
Some of these shops have recently become self-service—observe the other customers and follow their lead. If the proprietor serves you it is acceptable to point to the specific fruit or vegetable that you wish to purchase.

Pescheria or Fish Shop
The fish that passes for fresh in North America would turn up the nose of any smart Italian shopper. You won't find a vast selection, except in big cities, but the fish will be some of the best you have ever tasted. If you speak a smattering of Italian the proprietor can suggest some excellent preparation methods.

Roving markets

If you have ever been to open-air markets in the French countryside with their colourful displays of fabrics, vegetables, olives, artisanal cheeses, breads, and old-fashioned hand-made soaps, Italian markets will be a bit of a let down. Charm is not in abundance, with cheap clothing, shoe, and kitchenware stands outnumbering food stalls, but there are still treasures to be found. Most markets will have a few vegetable stalls, a couple of meat and salami carts, a shop with roasted chicken and pork, and a fish stand or two. Always patronize the stalls with the longest line-ups when buying perishables like meat and fish. As you will discover, the locals know a thing or two about quality and the extra wait is usually worth it. Fruit and vegetables are generally not self-service unless you see other people helping themselves. The owner or representative of your rental should be able to tell you the market days for the towns in your area. The hours are early, from 7 a.m. until 2 in the afternoon.

Supermarkets

In Italy, small family-run shops are sadly becoming a thing of the past and I encourage you to patronize them whenever possible. The convenience of a supermarket can't be beat, though, and the selection is often superb. Each region in Italy has its own supermarket chains, but in Tuscany there is a

Coop in almost every town, ranging in size from stores not much bigger than an *alimentari* to the fabulous Ipercoop (imagine a North American "big box" store with nothing but Italian products). Supermarkets are also indispensable when travelling with a group (just try to do two days worth of shopping for ten in a series of small shops and you'll see what I mean).

Some of the larger supermarkets are now open on Sundays and through the noon lunch break, but generally the hours are 9 a.m. to 1 p.m., and 4 to 8 p.m., five or six days a week. Check your local store for a closing day other than Sunday.

All supermarkets are approached in much the same manner and a little foreknowledge will help make your first experience less confusing:

Getting a shopping cart
To reduce cart theft most carts now require a 1 euro coin (refundable when you return the cart). The mechanism varies from store to store so you should watch another customer getting a cart and follow their lead.

Buying produce
You must bag and weigh your own produce. First look for the thin plastic gloves next to the produce section and place one on your hand. Drop your chosen item into the plastic bag provided and take the bag over to the scale. Place the bag on the weighing platform, look for the picture that corresponds to your item, and press the button. The machine will automatically weigh the produce and print out a sticker with the price. Place the sticker on the bag. Do not use the sticker to seal the bag—the scanning machine will not be able to read the bar code. Some products like oranges and onions will be pre-bagged and weighed. Occasionally there will be more than one variety of the same produce item, i.e. white and concord grapes—pay attention to the name of the product listed on the bin—it will usually be listed as such on the scale.

Buying from the meat, deli or fish counter
Many supermarkets have separate deli, fish and meat counters. There should be a number dispensing machine alongside—take a number and wait your turn. When your number is called you need to tell the server what and how much you want. Meat, fish, and deli products are often sold in units of 100 grams called *etti*. When you order, you can either ask for the total number of grams, i.e. 500 grams, *cinquecento grammi*, or much easier, 5 *etti*, *cinque etti*. The counter person will weigh and label the items, but you pay at the cashier when you leave.

Getting your bags and paying
Shopping bags are not provided free of charge so you must estimate the number of bags (*sachetti*) you will need and request them when the cashier begins scanning your items (i.e. *uno sacchetto, due sachetti, per favore*). You must also bag your own food. The total will appear on the cash register display. Correct change or the closest thing to it is always appreciated (a holdover from the *lira* days when coins were scarce—it was not uncommon in those days to receive penny candy in lieu of small change—no kidding!) Remember to bring your used bags for your next shopping trip.

Some recommended cookbooks

Italian cuisine as we think of it in North America doesn't really exist in Italy. All cooking is regional, based on those foods that are locally grown or produced. Most towns with even a few tourists will carry a cookbook or two in English but if you don't want to leave it up to chance you can bring a book with you from home. The following is a short list of my favourite Italian cookbooks—there are thousands more available. Take a trip to your local bookstore and browse until you find something that appeals to you. The following books may be ordered through your local independent bookseller or on the Internet.

All-purpose Italian

Cucina Fresca: Italian Food, Simply Prepared
by Viana La Place and Evan Kleiman, Morrow Cookbooks, 2001
> Happily back in print and one of the best cookbooks available for the holiday cook—most of the dishes can be made ahead of time and are relatively easy to prepare. *Cucina Rustica* and *Pasta Fresca* by the same authors are also highly recommended.

The Italian Country Table: Home Cooking from Italy's Farmhouse Kitchens
by Lynne Rossetto Kasper, Scribner, 1999
> Another splendid book with recipes for simple food with big flavours that can be made with ingredients found throughout the "boot". Just reading this book, with its wealth of cultural information and mouth-watering recipes, makes me want to jump on a plane to Italy.

Rome and Lazio

Cooking the Roman Way: Authentic Recipes from the Home Cooks and Trattorias of Rome
by David Downie, HarperCollins, 2002
> Delectable recipes for classics like *spaghetti carbonara, cacio e pepe,* and even the secret to making Jewish-style artichokes, the crispy fried thistle found on many Roman menus.

Diane Seed's Rome for All Seasons: A Cookbook
by Diane Seed, 10 Speed Press, 1996

> A beautifully illustrated soft cover book filled with this well-known cooking teacher's seasonal recipes. Somewhat difficult to find but always available through **www.abe.com**, a giant on-line used book database.

Emilia Romagna

The Splendid Table: Recipes from Emilia Romagna, the Heartland of Northern Italian Food
by Lynne Rossetto Kasper, Morrow Cookbooks, 1992

> When you glance through this book you'll be inclined to rent your next house in Emilia Romagna, if only to cook this fabulous food. It is a more complex regional cuisine and therefore the book contains some lengthier and more time-consuming recipes.

Tuscany

There are hundreds of Tuscan cookbooks in print, some excellent and some less so. If you prefer to buy a book in Italy, a number of good locally published books in English can be found on the shelves of most tourist town bookshops. Otherwise, here are a few recommendations:

Simply Tuscan: Recipes for a Well-lived Life
by Pino Luongo, Broadway Books, 2000

> Organized seasonally, this gorgeous book by the mastermind of "Tuscan Square", the indoor market/restaurant extravaganza in New York City, has terrific recipes that are fairly simple to prepare.

The Soul of Tuscany
Bon Appetit Special Collector's Edition, May 2000

> This issue of *Bon Appetit* magazine (their most popular ever) appeared just before we left Canada to rent a villa in Lastra a Signa, outside of Florence. Every recipe was a winner (especially the Panna Cotta with Strawberry-Vin Santo Sauce, the Porcini Frittata, and the Farro Salad) and most of the ingredients were in season and available. You can occasionally find a copy on eBay.

Liguria

Recipes from Paradise: Life and Food on the Italian Riviera
by Fred Plotkin, Little, Brown, 1997
> If you are lucky enough to find yourself a rental in Liguria, buy a copy of this book, read it from cover to cover for the wonderful history of the area, and take it along with you to Italy for the authentic recipes.

Sicily

Sicilian Home Cooking: Family Recipes from Gangivecchio
by Wanda and Giovanna Tornabene with Michele Evans, Knopf, 2001
> The follow-up to the fantastic *La Cucina Siciliana di Gangivecchio* in a smaller format with recipes geared more towards the home cook. The food is mouth-watering, and the narrative gives a fascinating insight into the author's life running a well-known restaurant on a historic estate.

Naples, Campania and the Amalfi Coast

Naples at Table: Cooking in Campania
by Arthur Schwartz, HarperCollins, 1998
> Arthur Schwartz brings the food of Campania to life in all its sun-kissed eggplant and tomato glory. Highly recommended.

❧

"Nothing significant exists under Italy's sun that is not touched by art. Its food is twice blessed because it is the product of two arts, the art of cooking and the art of eating."
MARCELLA HAZAN

Activities

There is so much to do on a trip to Italy — you are restricted only by your interests and financial resources (although some of the best activities like window shopping, wandering through historic towns and villages, and hiking through gorgeous countryside are absolutely free). Here are some ideas to pull you away from the usual rounds of sightseeing, museum visits, wine tasting and fine dining.

Hiking

Hiking is one of the best ways to experience a place. Walking old trade routes, country roads, and ancient pilgrims' trails allows you to imagine what it must have been like before the invention of the automobile when the average person's world ended at the next village. You have the opportunity to stop and chat with a farmer who proudly shows you his just-picked Sangiovese grapes, peer into a dilapidated medieval church, or get a close-up view of the wide variety of wild plants that grow along the roadways (not to mention the opportunity to burn off all those pasta meals). You'll have a real sense of arrival when you finally reach your destination.

My own experience hiking in Italy has been mainly in Tuscany and Umbria, expertly guided by a book called *Walking and Eating in Tuscany and Umbria* by James Ladsun and Pia Davis. I have found their directions highly detailed and accurate (except for a perilous descent in the autumn of 2003 to Sant' Antimo that left us with painful shins for days. There was an alternate route that we could have taken, not mentioned by the book, that would have been much less dangerous). About a dozen ring walks are described, but most of the walks require two cars to shuttle walkers back and forth between the beginning and end of the hike making most of these hikes only suitable for larger groups with more than one vehicle.

Another book, *Walking in Tuscany* by Gillian Price, has over 50 walks in Etruria, the ancient Etruscan stomping grounds that encompassed parts of Tuscany, Umbria and Lazio. With instructions a little less explicit than the Ladsun and Davis book, it is suitable for the more experienced hiker. She has some very interesting walks around Sorana and Pitigliano, an incredible undiscovered part of Tuscany near the Lazio border.

Both of these books are available through your local independent bookseller. Most small town tourist offices will be able to give you information on hiking in their area or put you in touch with a local hiking organization.

Some tips for hiking

- **Respect private property**. Many hiking trails pass through private land or very close to farmhouses. Move through quickly and keep voices low.

- **Wear proper footwear.** Lightweight hiking boots or very sturdy and comfortable walking shoes are recommended.

- **Take plenty of water** as well as a lunch and high-energy snacks.

- **Carry a lightweight umbrella** for sudden downpours.

- **In the autumn wear colourful clothing** to avoid making yourself a target for hunters.

Cooking classes

Renting a villa in Italy gives you the unprecedented opportunity to cook local dishes using local ingredients and experience Italian food as it was meant to be. If you have the time, money and interest I recommend spending a week at a residential cooking school before meeting up with your villa mates. Some villa owners can also arrange private cooking classes for you and a group of friends, taught by locals in your villa. Take a look at the excellent website for Shaw Guides, **www.shawguides.com**, for information on most of the cooking schools in operation in Italy today, ranging in price from about €1500 to over €5000 per week. (The more expensive courses are lead by food gurus like Marcella Hazan and Giuliano Bugialli.)

The following companies offer day classes that you can drive to from your rental:

DIVINA CUCINA

Judy Witts Francini provides superb hands-on one-, two- or three-day cooking classes in her adopted hometown of Florence. Her website is very informative with an interesting list of food artisans and a very reliable Florence restaurant review section.
www.divinacucina.com

GOOD TASTES OF TUSCANY

How about a day or two of cooking in the Villa Pandolfini, a renovated 13th-century villa in the hills outside of Florence in Lastra a Signa? Operated by Florence Villas (page 41), the cost of the class includes pick-up and drop-off in Florence.
www.tuscany-cooking-class.com

VACANZA ITALY

Along with a good selection of vacation rentals, Vacanza Italy offers one-day cooking classes in Florence, Lucca, Rome, Chianti and Ravello.
www.vacanzaitaly.com

THE INTERNATIONAL KITCHEN

This company offers a terrific selection of one-day cooking classes all over Italy, including Emilia Romagna, Sicily, the Veneto, Tuscany, Umbria and Rome. Some classes are conducted in private homes, others in restaurants. The website has a section for client feedback so you can be really sure that the course is right for you.
www.theinternationalkitchen.com

APICIUS

This Florentine cooking school specializes in week- and month-long programs for professionals and amateurs but will also organize day-long cooking, wine, and shopping classes for individuals and small groups.
www.apicius.it

Weddings

Italy has become a very popular wedding destination and the Internet overflows with agencies that specialize in organizing everything for the dream wedding. It is not as expensive as you might imagine, especially if you keep the guest list to a minimum, and combined with a villa stay, it adds up to a romantic event you will remember for a lifetime. Because it is such an important occasion, you must scrupulously check a company's references and be absolutely sure that you have all your paperwork together before you leave home. Italian bureaucrats have no sympathy for anyone without proper documentation.

Here are a few examples (once again, *caveat emptor*):

EUROEVENTS AND TRAVEL

Weddings almost anywhere in the country start at around €2700 for a budget civil wedding that includes paperwork, a bouquet for the bride, a photographer, and the agency fees, and go all the way up to an if-you-have-to-ask-you-can't-afford-it *Celebrity Package* which lays on all the luxuries: hairdressers, manicures and pedicures for the bridal party, limousine transportation, soprano or tenor for the ceremony, string quartet and six-piece band for the reception, five course dinner for 40 – 1400, a fireworks display, and optional bodyguard and helicopter transfers. The site has many letters of reference as well as e-mail addresses of real people you can contact for a reference.
www.destination-weddings-in-italy.com

WEDDINGS IN ITALY BY REGENCY

In business since 1990, this agency handles over 200 custom weddings a year in Florence and Tuscany, Rome, the Italian Riviera, the Amalfi Coast, and the Veneto. No prices are listed on their website although they do offer weddings in all price ranges. This is a company with a good reputation that has been written up in a number of publications, including *Time* magazine.
www.weddingsitaly.com

Shopping

Due to the global availability of Italian goods, Italy is not quite the shopper's paradise it once was but there is still a dizzying array of high quality fashion, shoes, ceramics, designer house wares, linens, and specialty foods at excellent prices. Label seekers can find their favourite designers at a discount in outlet centres.

Outlet shopping and discount stores

Outlet malls are starting to proliferate in Italy and they are generally still the real deal, offering seconds, samples and out of season clothing, instead of the cheap goods manufactured specifically for outlets that we find here in North America.

To get you started, here is a web page that lists numerous discount shops selling clothing, leather, linen and house wares:
www.made-in-italy.com/shopping/stores/stores.htm#florence

FOXTOWN
> If you are staying near Milan or Como (50 kilometres from Milan, 20 kilometres from Como), this outlet mall just across the border in Mendrisio, Switzerland has a dazzling assortment of clothing, shoes, linens and household goods. Their website has a good access map and lists all of the designers which include Versace, Gucci, Cerruti and Prada.
> www.foxtown.ch

THE MALL OUTLET CENTER
> This discount centre outside of Florence has fashion outlets by Gucci, YSL, Ungaro, Dolce & Gabbana and many others. The website gives information for shuttle bus service from Florence, driving directions, and directions by rail and taxi.
> www.outlet-firenze.com

SERRAVALLE OUTLET
> This is a huge outlet between Piemonte and Liguria not far from Genova with over 150 stores, designed in the style of an ersatz Ligurian village. A new centre has recently opened in the Castelli Romani, on the outskirts of Rome.
> www.mcarthurglen.it

The following books will help you in your search for goods that combine quality and value:

Suzy Gershman's Born to Shop Italy
by Suzy Gershman, Frommer, 2003
> The Italy edition of this popular and handy series gives information on the best deals, gift ideas, and even markets in the main tourist areas of Italy. It also includes hotel and restaurant recommendations.

Made in Italy: A Shopper's Guide to the Best of Italian Tradition
by Laura Morelli, Universe Publishing, 2003
> In the days of globalization it is refreshing to find a book that leads you to those tiny artisanal shops making one-of-a-kind items with an emphasis on quality.

Other things to buy

Linens
> Italy makes some of the most beautiful linens in the world, especially sheets, towels, bathrobes and kitchen linens.

Kitchen supplies
> Small designer kitchen goods make much-appreciated gifts. Products from famous designers like the whimsical Allessi are much cheaper in Italy than elsewhere.

Ceramic and terra cotta goods
> The best are found in Umbria, specifically in Gubbio and Deruta. Many shops will ship your purchases home for you.

Olive wood items
> A specialty of Tuscany—breadboards, wooden spoons, salad servers and bowls.

Jewellery
> Silver is an especially good buy.

Paper products
> Stationery, diaries, menu cards, address and blank books.

Leather goods

Shoes, jackets, high-fashion clothing, handbags and leather-bound books.

Fine Wines and Liqueurs

Each region has its own specialties.

Food Items

A cornucopia of good things, ranging from olive oil to condiments to cookies to sauces to dried pasta. Check with your country's customs agency before you import meat or cheese. In Canada and the U.S., most meat and cheese imports are forbidden. You will be subject to a hefty fine and confiscation if you try to smuggle your treasures home. The cute little dogs you see at airports these days have very sensitive noses.

Guidebooks

I am a guidebook junkie. I buy guides to places I'm sure I will never see just to get a taste of the sights, sounds and flavours of a new and exotic locale. There are plenty of terrific guides to Italy, but only a few of them are really worth carrying with you on your travels. Much of the information can be read and absorbed ahead of time leaving you to tear out and discard the sections you don't need — guidebooks become outdated quickly and have little value in the second hand market. The following are some of the tried and true:

Cadogan

Cadogan guides, published in Britain, are a traveller's best friend. In-depth and detailed, opinionated and quite funny, they are a joy to read even if you are not planning a trip right away. They cover some of the undiscovered parts of Italy like Emilia Romagna, Sardinia, Abruzzo and Molise, and their hotel and restaurant recommendations are excellent, if a bit lean in the budget category.

Available guides:

Central Italy (Rome, Lazio, Abruzzo and Molise)
Bay of Naples & Southern Italy (includes Capri and the Amalfi Coast)
Bologna & Emilia Romagna
Florence
Italian Riviera
Lombardy & the Italian Lakes (including Milan)
Milan
Northeast Italy (includes the Veneto, Venice and Lake Garda)
Rome City Guide
Rome & the Heart of Italy
Rome, Venice, Florence
Sardinia
Sicily
Tuscany
Tuscany, Umbria & the Marches
Umbria
Venice

Frommer's

I have great affection for this series. The very first trip I ever took was with *Frommer's Europe on $20 a Day* (I fear that dates me). On that excursion, I barely let my "bible" out of my sight, following its advice to the letter. *Frommer's* has changed since then—they now have hundreds of titles, a useful website, www.frommers.com, and *$15 a Day* has become *$70 a Day*. They are reasonably good overall guides, covering much of Italy, if somewhat lacking in panache.

Available guides:

Florence, Tuscany & Umbria
Irreverent Guide to Rome
Italy
Italy From $70 a Day
Italy's Best-Loved Driving Tours
Northern Italy's Best-Loved Driving Tours
*Northern Italy (includes Venice, the Dolomites, South Tirol, Milan and
    Lombardy, Liguria and the Italian Riviera)*
Portable Florence
Portable Venice
Rome, Past & Present
Rome
Tuscany & Umbria's Best-Loved Driving Tours
Tuscany & Umbria
Hanging out in Italy (geared for "young, adventurous, hip travellers")
Italy for Dummies
Suzy Gershman's Born to Shop Italy

Fodor's

This venerable guide has been around forever and contains plenty of detailed information geared to the American traveller. Their website www.fodors.com is very useful, especially the forums, and the on-line restaurant and hotel reviews.

Available guides:

Italy
See It Italy
Upclose Italy
Around Rome with Kids

(Fodor's cont.)

Pocket Rome
Rome
Citypack Venice
Citypack Rome's Best
Citypack Florence's Best
Exploring Tuscany
Florence, Tuscany and Umbria
Naples, Capri, and the Amalfi Coast
Venice and the Veneto
Venice: The Collected Traveller
Central Italy: The Collected Traveller: Tuscany and Umbria

Time Out

These British guides are younger, hipper and generally more sophisticated than any other guidebook series, but still include recommendations in all price ranges. Opinionated and not afraid to tell the truth about the over-hyped and over-rated, they give you plenty of cultural information and insight into the modern political and social life of Italy. Unlike most guide books, the hotel and restaurant recommendations change quite dramatically from year to year, giving frequent travellers plenty of new, and for the most part excellent, choices.

Available guides:

Florence and the Best of Tuscany
Naples, Capri, Sorrento and the Amalfi Coast
Rome
Venice, Verona, Treviso and the Veneto
Rome: Eating and Drinking Guide
Rome: City Guide

Rough Guides

There is nothing particularly rough about these excellent guides. They don't cover as many areas of Italy as *Cadogan* but they are very comprehensive and offer recommendations in all budget categories. The guidebooks are well organized, easy to use, and contain detailed maps of towns and villages. Highly recommended as an all-round guide.

Available guides:

Italy
Rome (pocket size, also available as an e-book)
Sardinia
Sicily
Tuscany and Umbria
Venice and the Veneto

Eyewitness

Eyewitness Guides are my preferred armchair travel guides, but they are still worth packing on any trip that takes you to Rome, Florence or Venice. Crammed with photos, maps and interesting facts, they are a godsend for walkers, leading you through typical neighbourhoods and undiscovered corners of the city, pointing out art and architectural features along the way. Hotel and restaurant information in the back of each book is concise but a little short on budget options.

Available guides:

Top 10: Tuscany
Top 10: Venice
Top 10: Rome
Top 10: Sicily
A Taste of Tuscany (guide to Tuscan food)
Italy
Rome
Florence and Tuscany
Venice and the Veneto
Milan and the Lakes
Sicily
Sardinia
Naples

Rick Steves

Rick Steves is a runaway success, at least judging from the large number of tourists I saw on my last trip to Italy clutching his book like a talisman. Rick gently coaxes people who may have only travelled on a package tour in the past into getting off the beaten track and discovering the real Italy. He leads you by the hand through the sights and gives plenty of insider tips on how to avoid common tourist rip-offs, find an inexpensive but delicious meal in a typical trattoria, and steer clear of long museum queues. His historical and cultural information is somewhat superficial (he can't do everything well) and his overall popularity has brought crowds to some previously undiscovered spots like the Cinque Terre in Liguria.

Available guides:

Italy
Venice
Rome
Florence/Tuscany

Michelin

The revered *Michelin Red Guide Italia* is available only in Italian, but is not difficult to decipher once you become familiar with the layout. This is not the guide for people like me who love long mouth-watering descriptions of restaurant food, but it offers an abundant choice of inns and eating places throughout Italy. For historical and sightseeing information the *Green Guides* can't be beat and they now contain a smattering of hotel and restaurant recommendations, although not enough to place them in the all-round guide category.

Available guides:

Red Guide: Italia (Italian language only)
Green Guide: Italy
Green Guide: Tuscany
Green Guide: Sicily
Green Guide: Venice
Green Guide: Rome

Lonely Planet

This company has only recently started covering Europe after many years of publishing the definitive guides to Asia, Africa and South America. These no-nonsense guides tend to be geared to the younger traveller getting around mostly by train and bus, but contain hotel and restaurant listings in all price categories. *Lonely Planet* is not yet a leader in this crowded field but is certainly a series to watch in the future.

Available guides:

Italy
Tuscany and Umbria
Venice
Rome
Florence
Walking in Italy
Cycling Italy
Sardinia
Sicily
World Food Italy
Italian Phrasebook

Arrivaderci, Italia

We rise at 5 a.m. and creep into the kitchen to avoid waking the others. While coffee is brewing I strip the sheets from the beds, leaving them in the entranceway for the caretaker. After a few sips of espresso it is time to leave. We close the door quietly behind us and look back at the fine villa that has been our home for the past two weeks. As we start out, the still autumn air is almost cold and patches of fog lie heavily on the fields. The sun has not yet risen, but the moon is full and the road is so devoid of traffic that we switch off the headlights for a moment to fully appreciate the silence and exquisite light. We reach Chiusi and the rail station far too soon. I park the car in the lot next to the rental agency and drop the keys through the slot in the door of the adjacent café. The train arrives just as the sun is starting to peek over the horizon and as I board the train thoughts of work, home, and the day-to-day responsibilities of my life start to sneak into my consciousness. By the time we pull into Rome and transfer to the train that will take us to the airport I have accepted that another extraordinary holiday has ended but I am consoled by the knowledge that memories created on this journey will sustain me for months to come. In fact, I am already planning my next trip…perhaps a beach house in Sicily, a mountain chalet in Trentino, or a farmhouse in Emilia Romagna…

Equipped with the information in this book I hope you now have the confidence to plan your own Italian dream vacation. Your trip will reflect your individuality and will be imbued with all the spontaneity that a holiday like this deserves. Your memories will be your finest souvenirs. *Buon Viaggio!*

"In the heart of every man, wherever he is born…there is one small corner which is Italian, that part which finds regimentation irksome, the dangers of war frightening, strict morality stifling, that part which loves frivolous and entertaining art, admires larger-than-life solitary heroes, and dreams of an impossible liberation from the strictures of a tidy existence."

LUIGI BARZINI

Useful Web Addresses

Train schedules, reservations and tickets

www.trenitalia.it
The website of the Italian national railways has on-line schedules, but no mechanism for buying tickets from overseas.

www.raileurope.com
You can make reservations and purchase tickets on-line through this site for most of the major Italian rail routes but be aware that the tickets are more expensive than those purchased in Italy.

Weather reports, currency conversion and travel advisories

www.italy-weather-and-maps.com
Weather reports and maps for Italy

www.seekitaly.com/news/from_roma.html
A Rome-based site that lists upcoming strikes and current travel advisories

www.timeanddate.com/worldclock
A world clock showing the present time in Italy

www.xe.com/ucc
The Universal Currency Converter

Museum reservations

www.weekendafirenze.com
Offers advance reservations (for a fee) for the Uffizi Gallery, Accademia Gallery and the incredible Vasari Corridor in Florence

www.culturalitaly.com
Advance reservations for Venice's Doges Palace "Secret Itineraries Tour", a highlight of my last trip to Venice. The tour takes you through the secret back corridors of the palace, into the torture chambers and up into the rafters. You can also book tickets for the famous Palio horse race in Siena.

Restaurant and food information

www.slowfood.com
This highly respected Italian organization promotes food artisans and a
return to traditional food culture. The site contains some restaurant
recommendations and sells guidebooks to restaurants as well as regional
cookbooks (mostly in Italian).

www.winespectator.com
A comprehensive wine site with plenty of information on Italian wines to
help you organize your wine tasting excursions before you leave home

www.italianfood.about.com
A fabulous authentic Italian recipe database and an informative free
newsletter

www.lacucinaeoliana.com
Absolutely mouth-watering recipes from Sicily and the Aeolian Islands

www.mangiarebene.net
The English language version of one of Italy's most popular recipe websites

www.egullet.com
Excellent Italian restaurant information in their forums

www.cucinait.com/world/home_we.asp
The on-line English language version of *Cucina Italiana* (the foremost Italian
cooking magazine)

Car rental

www.autoeurope.com
Very reliable discount car rental agency with excellent prices and on-line
booking

Day tours (including hiking and cycling)

www.accidentaltourist.com
Day walking, cycling and cooking tours at an estate outside of Florence

www.cicloposse.com
Day cycling trips in Tuscany starting at €150 per person, including bicycle
rental and lunch

www.initaly.com/ads/hike/hike.htm
Private guided walks in Southern Tuscany

www.actividayz.com
Local farm visits, winery tours, truffle hunting, cooking and hiking,
throughout Italy, operated by The Parker Company

www.cinqueterre.it/en/cta1.html
Good over all website for the Cinque Terre includes maps and descriptions
of the trail system

Vacation rentals and hotels (including reviews)

www.tripadvisor.com
Hotel reviews

www.venere.com
The best hotel site for Italy includes reviews and on-line availability check.

www.slowtrav.com
A comprehensive site for the vacation renter: vacation rental reviews,
agency reviews and information on just about everything else related to
Italian travel. Excellent message board at www.slowtalk.com

www.initaly.com
Information on accommodation (vacation rentals and hotels), regions,
festivals, sightseeing, and some interesting tours. A must before any trip to
Italy

www.emmeti.it/index.uk.html
Everything about Italy for the tourist: hotels, restaurants, museums and
sightseeing

(Vacation rentals and hotels cont.)

www.agriturismo.com
Over 1000 listings for vacation rentals on farms, including a good selection of wheelchair accessible properties

Cooking and language classes

www.koinecenter.com
Language classes in Florence, Lucca, Cortona, Orbetello and Bologna with classes from one week to many months. They also offer art and cooking courses combined with language classes.

www.newitineraries.it
A company that organizes reasonably priced week-long language classes, and language and cooking home stays in teachers' homes, inclusive of meals, accommodation, tuition and excursions.

www.italycookingschools.com
"Mama Margaret Cooking Holidays" has cooking classes for all budgets throughout Italy.

www.shawguides.com
Comprehensive listing of recreational cooking and wine schools in Italy

About the author

Lynn Jennings fell head over heels in love with Italy on her first trip there at age seventeen. Between trips to Italy, this professionally trained chef has found the time to live in France and Japan, and travel extensively in Europe and Asia. She divides her time between Vancouver and the Southern Gulf Islands, where she writes about food and travel.

ISBN 141203945-2

9 781412 039451